A LIFE REBUILT

A LIFE REBUILT

*The Remarkable Transformation
of a War Orphan*

SYLVIA RUTH GUTMANN

EPIGRAPH BOOKS
RHINEBECK, NEW YORK

Paperback ISBN: 978-1-944037-94-9
Hardcover ISBN: 978-1-944037-95-6
eBook ISBN: 978-1-944037-96-3
Library of Congress Control Number: 2018933432

Book design by Colin Rolfe.

Epigraph Books
22 East Market Street, Suite 304
Rhinebeck, New York 12572
(845) 876-4861
www.EpigraphPS.com

For Mali and Nathan Gutmann and my sister Rita

who gave me everything including this story

"Never, never, never give up."

—Winston Churchill

"Home is the land of one's childhood and youth. Whoever has lost it remains lost himself, even if he has learned not to stumble."

—Jean Améry, Holocaust survivor and author of *At The Mind's Limits*

AUTHOR'S NOTE

It is not an exaggeration to say that I have been writing this book all my life. Many of the conversations and the scenes that I write about have spanned decades ago. I have reconstructed them to the best of my ability in the way I remember them.

TABLE OF CONTENTS

Prologue   XVII

PART ONE: LOST

1. Life Interrupted   3
2. Growing Up   7
3. Daddy Sam   12
4. Princess Bride   16
5. Love and Loss   18
6. Castaway   21
7. Tango   26
8. No More Teachers No More Books   29
9. Doomed   32
10. Someday My Prince Will Come   38

PART TWO: AFTERMATH

11. Damage Control   43
12. Memory Keeper   45
13. My Baby Boy   48
14. The Loony Bin and Me   53

15. Dr. Bob   58

16. His Madonna   62

17. A Small Seed of Growth   67

18. War Stories   73

19. We Are Warriors   78

20. Identity Issues   82

21. Once Upon a Time   85

22. My Prince   97

23. Fallen Hero   101

24. Proof of Angels   106

25. Homeless   110

26. Love and Memory   113

27. Mr. Wrong   117

28. Awakening   120

29. Because I Remember Love   125

30. You Before Me   129

31. The Butterfly Effect   134

32. Two To Tango   141

33. How To Say Good-bye   151

34. My German Connection   154

PART THREE: FOUND

35. Breaking the Silence   159

36. Long Ago and Far Away   166

37. Back to Before   172

38. Hero In Chanel   180

39. Up Close and Evil   190

40. Love and Other Difficulties   196

41. My Own Berlin   207

42. Facing History   211
43. A New World of Love   221
44. Out of Hiding   229
45. My Father's Voice   233
46. Sealed in Stone   238
47. Empty Rooms   251
48. Family Ties   257
49. Paper Clips   266
50. A Voyage Of The Heart   275

PROLOGUE

"Go back to the barrack, my sweet girls. I'll be back soon!" Mama shouted from her place in line.

I ran to her calling, "Mama, Mama, take me with you!"

"Rita!" she shouted. "Please take care of Sylvie. Promise me you'll take care of the baby."

It is 1942. I am a three-year-old prisoner in the French Vichy-run internment camp at Rivesaltes. I have no memory of that time, but according to my late sister Rita, one day there was a 3 a.m. roll call. Mama came into the children's barrack to dress my two older sisters and me then told us to wait outside. She had been ordered to collect her meager belongings for the "trip to the work camp" in the East.

This is all she had time to say to my ten-year-old sister before the French guards pushed my mother onto the waiting cattle car to Auschwitz. My brave mother knew nothing about the thousands of deportations that would come later—nor could she have ever imagined the Final Solution. In the face of the unknown, Mama had made a heart-wrenching choice to leave us behind with a stranger who had promised to save our lives.

My mother's brutal and swift departure left me in limbo. It forever changed the ways in which I responded to the world around me.

The incomprehensible rupture of that moment altered the normal ways in which I should have thought about love and intimacy. It ripped to shreds the ways in which I should have felt about home, motherhood, friendship, and my responsibility to others and myself.

Deeply traumatized, desperately bereaved, and draped in loss, I arrived with my two older sisters in New York in 1946. I was seven. I had lost my parents, my language, and my home. I grew up surrounded by a conspiracy of silence and shame. America said, "You have to erase from your memory everything that happened to you. Put all that behind you. Hide your grief. Fit in. Be normal. Move on." To be normal and to fit in, I surrendered my past, my history, and my memory. I shut down. I became numb to my feelings. I could not move on.

These messages of shame and silence erased my life. I grew up believing that who I was was not good enough. I had no identity, so I had to make one up. That split in me would be the cause of pain and conflict for the next forty years of my life.

Melanie Klein, the late Austrian-British psychologist, wrote that when a child goes through a state of mind comparable to mourning, this mourning is revived whenever that grief is experienced in later life.

My beloved sister Rita, a surrogate mother and the storyteller of my forgotten early life, died in 1993. I had a post-traumatic stress breakdown and tried to end my life. I was fifty-four. With the help of my kind, wise therapist, I finally allowed myself to grieve. My mother's early departure from my life and the loss of my memory had deeply impacted the way I lived in the world.

I moved through the world in a state of numbness and shock. I worried about school, about my teachers, about never quite catching up, about my abusive aunt, about being accepted, about not belonging and feeling lost and alone—not just as a child, but throughout most of my life.

I was sixty-two when I concluded a journey that had taken thirty-five years, three countries, and thousands of miles to make. It would recreate the most important scene in my life— the day my mother left me.

These pages narrate the story of what happened to my family and to me, and my lifelong climb out of silence and shame. This is the story of how the Holocaust became the ground on which I finally built an authentic, full, and happy life.

PART I
Lost

CHAPTER ONE

LIFE INTERRUPTED

This is my earliest memory: I am seven years old and sailing to America on the *Athos II*, a large, ugly, crowded ship. It still smells like the cattle it had once carried to slaughter. Babies are crying and people are shouting in languages I don't understand. We live in the hold of the ship near the rotten vegetables, all the women and children in one big room. Instead of beds we sleep in hammocks, three stacked to a row. My sister Rita, now fourteen, sleeps on top; I sleep in the middle; and Susi, age thirteen, sleeps in the hammock under me.

The boat pitches and rolls. I throw up and pee in my hammock. Now my dress stinks, my socks stink, my hair stinks, my mouth stinks, and my underpants stink. I am just a stinking little girl.

Unlike the other orphans on the ship, we do not have an escort or a member of a rescue organization to supervise us. We are alone. I never know where my two sisters are, so I roam alone on the deck every day clutching my doll. After we were smuggled into Switzerland in 1943, I was separated from my sisters for a time. I was sent to live with my Tante Rosa, Papa's sister, in Zurich. A kind social worker from the Swiss Aid Committee for Immigrant Children gave me the doll when she removed me from a mountain family whom she suspected of abuse and neglect. This is where Aunt Rosa had selfishly and secretly sent me.

To every woman on the ship who looks kindly at me, I plead, "Will you be my mommy? Please be my mommy!"

We arrive in New York Harbor after enduring three weeks on an unusually stormy sea. Hundreds of weary, helpless people, all of them Jewish refugees and survivors of the Holocaust like us, are told by the French crew that there is a longshoremen's strike and that we are not allowed to leave the ship until it is over.

Two days later, I watch as a tugboat comes toward us. It pulls up alongside the ship and I see a crowd of people waving. As they climb on board, I watch a short, bald man with a wide smile look around. He is calling out the names of my sisters and me. He does not know what we look like, so we raise our arms and wave.

Carrying a large straw basket under his arm and holding the hand of a beautiful, dark-haired, smiling woman with cobalt blue eyes, he says in German, "Hello! I am your mother's brother, your Uncle Sam, and this is my wife, your Aunt Gerdy." Quickly reaching into the basket, he places a small wrapped package in my hand and motions for me to open my gift.

It's two slices of bread, top and bottom layered with mayonnaise, lettuce and tomato, and wrapped in a strange paper that crinkles and slides. "Wax paper," Uncle Sam calls it. I have never seen bread that is white. Nor have I tasted anything as delicious as this sandwich! At the sight of my tomato-splattered dress, my mouth and cheeks covered in mayonnaise, my uncle laughs and unwraps another sandwich for me. Afraid that he might take it away, I hold it tightly, smacking my lips and humming quietly in between hurried bites. I cannot summon up a single memory of my sisters in this scene—yet I can remember the precise taste of that sandwich, the satisfying flavor of the white bread thickly spread with creamy American mayonnaise.

I love him right away. Every day that week, Uncle Sam and his wife bring us new and delicious food treats. Then one morning as I watch the familiar tugboat pull up, Uncle Sam is alone and there is no straw basket under his arm. He has come to take us home.

I step off the boat on April 9, 1946, with my Uncle Sam and my two teenage sisters. The day is warm, the sky is cloudless, and the streets are full of people and cars. The immigration officers rename us "Goodman" when they stamp our papers. To get to my uncle and aunt's apartment house at 645 Fort Washington Avenue, we walk past a candy store where a crowd of teenagers, like my sisters, are drinking what looks like milk through a straw. Three years later I will discover that delicious vanilla egg cream for myself. We walk past an F. W. Woolworth and an island of cobblestones where women with baby carriages sit on green wooden benches alongside a long black iron fence in the middle of Broadway amid the roar of morning traffic. As we are led into our relatives' apartment, Uncle Sam takes me to a door that opens into a dark room. When he turns on the light, I see a small boy with light blond hair. The boy rubs his eyes open to look at me. I am afraid that he will cry when he opens his mouth, but instead, a wide, open smile crosses his face as he reaches out his tiny hand to me.

I have been welcomed! He has won my heart. His name is Michel and he is three years old. He and his newborn brother, Stuart, are my first cousins.

Uncle Sam and his wife Gerdy decided months before our arrival that because Rita is the oldest of us three girls, she will live with them to help take care of Michel, Stuart, and me.

My sister Susi is delivered to the home of Aunt Ella, the elder of Papa's two surviving sisters. She is a widow who lives on 179th and Broadway, one short subway stop away from Rita and me.

Several days after we arrive, I cannot control the scratching from the lice that I caught on board the ship that brought me to America. I lean my face forward over the kitchen sink. The liquid that Aunt Gerdy pours on my scalp smells a little like my hammock and the bathroom on the ship. Wrapping a towel around my head, Gerdy tells me the liquid will have to stay on a while. I walk back into the bedroom I share with Michel and, with my eyes tearing and my scalp burning, sit on my bed. Michel is squeezing his nose and making a silly face. Thinking that he is angry because of the smell, I stand up and walk to the window. After what seems like a very long time, Gerdy unwraps the towel. She slowly runs a fine-toothed black plastic comb through my hair, starting at my hot and burning scalp, section by section, removing the nits.

The bedroom window of our ground-floor apartment is eye level to the sidewalk and now that it has become dark outside, the ceiling light in the room draws attention to this dreadful scene. When she holds the comb up to the light looking for the dead nits, I see that a small group of people has gathered outside. They are staring at a dark-haired, skinny, frightened young girl with tears running down her face. Although I do not yet speak English, somehow I understand by their looks of pity that this is a moment of deep humiliation and shame.

CHAPTER TWO

GROWING UP

Not knowing a word of English, Rita and Susi are enrolled in Junior High School 164. I am put into the second grade at PS 169. It is a large, white, Gothic-like brick-and-mortar building with dirty, worn stairs and hallways that mysteriously take me into the cafeteria or the girls' locker room or the auditorium that sometimes doubles as the gym.

I was nearly four when my sisters and I were smuggled into Switzerland after our parents were deported to Auschwitz. I was seven when we came to America and I had never been to school. With no help or special tutoring to learn the skills I should already have, it becomes impossible for me to keep up with the rest of my second-grade class, though I take to English right away. I like hearing the sound of my own voice, but most other subjects are confusing. Math in particular is excruciating. So I sit in the back of the room hoping that I will not be called on.

My desk is in the row next to the windows, where I sit and daydream that I am outside playing in the park across the street. On one beautiful sunny day as I am gazing out at the trees, a howling sound catches my attention. I stand up to look down at the sidewalk where I see two dogs that are stuck together. They sound like they are screaming in pain, trying to pull themselves apart from one another. I have never seen a sight like this before and it frightens me.

"Mrs. Lynch! Mrs. Lynch! Look! There are two dogs stuck together and they are hurt! Please let's go and pull them apart!" I yell.

All the kids have left their seats and come running over to look at what I have discovered. Mrs. Lynch approaches, her face bright red, and without even glancing out the window, she orders the children to sit down and be still. Muttering something about "those damn foreigners," she banishes me from the room while all the kids laugh.

Every week we have "show and tell." I love this hour. It's the only time that I don't have to disappear to the back of the room. We work on our projects all week long in preparation for that one hour. This week I plan to show the rose-colored dress I wore on the ship that brought me to America.

When it's finally my turn, I hold up the dress and I stand in front of my class.

"I was born in Belgium. My name was really Ruth. It sounded too Jewish, so I was called Sylvie," I say. "My real mama and papa went away and they were killed. I came here on a big, smelly boat and I threw up and did pee-pee in my hammock where I slept."

From out of nowhere, Mrs. Lynch is next to me. She grabs my arm, swings me around to face her, and points a finger in my face. In a loud, angry voice she says, "You little liar! Be quiet right now! Go sit down!"

I look down at the floor as I walk to my seat in the back of the room. And I never talk about it again.

* * *

I am far behind my class in math. Mrs. Lynch has warned my aunt that if I don't catch up, I will have to repeat second grade. It's a hot August morning. I am eight years old and as I have done every morning during summer recess, I sit at the brown, vinyl-covered card table in the bedroom that I share with my cousin Michel and wait for Aunt Gerdy.

"What is two times four?" Gerdy asks.

"Eight," I say.

"What is three times four?"

"Twelve," I say.

"What is three times three?"

"Nine," I quickly reply.

"What is four times six?" *Four times six, four times six, four times six.* I can see the page I have memorized in my head, 4×6 = ___, but where is the answer? I look for the answer. I can't see it. My heart is pounding in my ears. Aunt Gerdy has a bad temper. Every cell in my body is lit up in fear. I wish I could just disappear.

Gerdy's face is twisted with rage; her anger is out of control. Hands that seem to have a life of their own smack my face, my arms, and my head. "You should have learned this already. We've been going over it every day. School starts next week, and I'm warning you right now. Mrs. Lynch better not call me to school again. You better have this memorized," Gerdy threatens as she leaves the room.

Tears trace a path down my face and my whole body shakes as I put my head and burning face down on my arms and cry. *I hate you, Gerdy.*

* * *

Barbara May is my first friend. She is one year younger than me and she shares everything with me—her dolls, her books, her hair ribbons, her lunch, her clothes, and her mother, Elsie, who is a Jewish refugee from Hitler's Germany and Aunt Gerdy's best friend. The family lives on the sixth floor, and for a short time Elsie is a concerned witness of my new life. She is my refuge, a giver of missing and needed smiles, hugs, love, comfort, and understanding that I do not get from my aunt.

Today, I will sneak Aunt Gerdy's bracelet into my school bag. She never wears it. I love the bright green stones. My aunt won't even know that it's missing. I plan to put it right back into her jewelry box as soon as I come home from school, but I forget and she sees it on my wrist.

"Why are you wearing my bracelet?" Gerdy asks.

"It's not yours," I lie. "I found it on the sidewalk in front of school."

Gerdy pulls me into the bedroom and over to the black art deco vanity. She opens her jewelry box and points to where the missing bracelet should be. "You're lying, Sylvia!"

I am too afraid now to admit the truth, so I keep insisting that I found it. By now Gerdy has gone wild, screaming and hitting me on the head and arms with a wooden cooking spoon.

I hold my hands up to try and stop the blows from hitting my head and face. I run from the room and toward the front door, when Elsie enters.

"Gerdy, what are you doing? Stop this. She's only nine years old. Don't scream and hit her all the time. Let her be a child!"

* * *

Every day after I come home from school, I walk into our bedroom, pick up the doll that the kind social worker in Switzerland gave me, and hold her in my arms. I whisper softly, "Your mommy's home." I always call her "my little girl." She is about two feet tall with a delicate porcelain face, a small red Cupid's bow mouth, bright blue glass eyes that look real, and a long black-and-white taffeta dress. I bathe and comb her shiny black hair, and then I smother her with hugs and kisses.

One day after school, I rush into the bedroom, excited to practice my English with her, and I see that my doll is not sitting on my bed. I panic, because this is where I always leave her, and so I begin to search the room. I am looking under the cover of my bed when I hear Aunt Gerdy walk up behind me.

"Are you looking for your dirty, beat-up looking doll?" she snarls. "I threw her away. Now change your clothes and go sweep the floor."

I won't cry. Gerdy doesn't like it when I cry. "Stop crying or I'll give you something to really cry about," she would threaten.

On my birthday, she gives me a brand-new doll. I never play with her. She is small, clean, and neat with fake blond hair, painted pink cheeks, and eyes that are just doll's eyes. She isn't my little girl. We have no history together. She does not need a mommy.

CHAPTER THREE

DADDY SAM

My Uncle Sam loves me. I call him "Daddy." Sunday morning is when Aunt Gerdy goes to her sisterhood meetings at the Hebrew Tabernacle, leaving Daddy and me alone. That is when he tells me about his boyhood in Fürth, Germany—and when he tells me about my mother.

"Chantal, the oldest of the five girls, was the real beauty, but your mother, Mali, the youngest, with her flaming red hair, was my favorite."

Not a Sunday goes by that he does not tell me the soccer story. "I loved soccer. Once a week I would sneak out to the soccer field to play with the local high school boys who were all twice as old as me. One day our strict, Orthodox, Torah-studying Polish-German father caught Mali sitting in the kitchen, bent over a small pile of study books doing my homework. She told him that she had sent me on an important errand and that I had agreed to do it if she would do my homework. He accused her of lying, but she did not back down even though they both knew he was right. So he punished her. Mali was like a mother to me."

Because Daddy Sam left Germany and came to America in 1935, he was gone when his beloved sister Mali gave birth to me. So this is all he ever tells me about my mother.

Daddy has his own business, Sam Kleinman Furs, on West 72nd Street. His shop on the second floor is where he styles, cuts, sews, and fits his clients' jackets and coats. A big picture window faces the street, directly over the liquor store. Next door is The Royale, a busy bakery.

Friday night is the only time Daddy Sam comes home in time to eat with us. Gerdy wears bright red lipstick and red rouge on her cheeks. Light blue eye shadow is brushed on her lids, and brown pencil fills in her thin eyebrows tonight. Gold clip-on earrings from the F. W. Woolworth store hang from her ears. Her hair was washed and styled at the hairdresser earlier in the day. The scent of Nina Ricci cologne fills the air.

When Daddy Sam arrives he holds in his hand the familiar white Bloom's bakery box. It holds my favorite treat, chocolate layer cake. In his pockets are the three Almond Joy chocolate candy bars he pretends to hide from Michel, Stuart, and me.

I am smacking my lips and humming while I eat when I think about another evening so different than this. It is played out every Wednesday, when I sit for hours choking and dry heaving as Gerdy stands watch. "Eat your food," she demands. Boiled fish topped with boiled onion. I hate onion. I want to throw up from the smell so I pick at the fish. When Gerdy sees that I have pushed the onions aside, she screams, "We will sit here all night." I am sobbing, gagging, and trying not to throw up when I hear Daddy Sam's key in the door. "Gerdy, it's ten o'clock. Look at her. She's dead tired. That's enough."

Aunt Gerdy is disagreeable and sharp-tongued almost every night. Tonight she is happy, and warm. Her husband is home.

How I love Friday nights!

* * *

Daddy works from early morning until late at night, six days a week. He is off on Sundays, when we all go to Randall Island to watch him play soccer. He is a fierce competitor, agile and skilled. He kicks the ball and sometimes even hits it with his head. I'm afraid that he will hurt his head. My daddy has no hair.

Many years later, he tells me that he had played professionally for the Maccabees, a well-known German-Jewish team, before he was forced to flee Germany. My happiest moments on those special Sundays are when Daddy would find a way to sneak to the sidelines during the game and give me a hug or a kiss on the cheek or a whispered "I love you." I am his special little girl, maybe his only connection to his own beloved sister. After the game, we always go to Orner's German-American restaurant on Broadway and 164th Street to eat deviled eggs, sweet-and-sour cucumber salad, and roast potatoes with pot roast.

Rita is sixteen when she quits George Washington High School. The Hebrew Immigrant Aid Society pays the tuition to the Hollywood School of Beauty. When she graduates eight months later, the school finds her a hairdressing job in a small shop on 181st and Broadway, not far from where she lives with Sam, Gerdy, Michel, Stuart, and me.

Five months later, Sam and Gerdy tell her that now that she has a job, the Hebrew Immigrant Aid Society will no longer pay for her room and board. Sam tells her that she will have to pay it out of her salary. Because she sleeps on the sofa in the living room and rarely has more than a cup of coffee before she leaves for work, she looks for a new place to live. She asks her friend Marian, an orphaned teenager she met on the ship that carried us to America, to share the studio apartment that she has found near her work.

Rita is leaving. She has packed all her belongings into three small suitcases that Marian's boyfriend will pick up in his car. It's a crisp fall afternoon when I sit down with my lovely sister. I am scared. I feel strange emotions suddenly rising in me. I don't quite know what they are—anger, sorrow? Somehow it's all too much. *Take me. Take me, please. Don't leave me*, I want to plead. Rita is crying. It makes me cry too. She folds me in her arms and in a hoarse whisper, says, "Always show Sam and Gerdy how grateful you are to them for bringing us here. Be a good girl. Listen to Aunt Gerdy. Don't make her mad. Otherwise they might make you leave, too. And you have nowhere else to go."

My first memories with Rita in Washington Heights with Gerdy and Sam are fractured and brief, glimmers of that time, but that's how they all are. It's always Gerdy's rage that I will remember the most.

Daddy and I spend a lot of time alone together during those early years. We talk about school, my friends, and if I am happy living with them. "Yes," I tell him. I love my daddy and I don't want to hurt his feelings, so I lie. I am not happy. I am confused and angry. No matter how much I clean and iron, I can never please her. She is never happy with me. Sometimes I just want to run away.

CHAPTER FOUR

PRINCESS BRIDE

Aunt Edith, our father's sister, soon learns that Rita is being courted by Ralph, her much-married, charming, Puerto Rican boss at the beauty salon where she works. Edith is determined to get Rita out of New York and to end this budding romance. Aunt Edith invites her to her home in Cleveland, Ohio. That's where Jack lives. He's the handsome, twenty-three-year-old Holocaust survivor who Aunt Edith knows will be a perfect match for her favorite niece. When they first meet, Jack walks up the hill to Edith's house, wearing his Air Force uniform and carrying a bouquet of flowers. He waves hello to my nineteen-year-old sister Rita, his future bride.

Jack's foster mother, Mrs. Winfred Fryer, is a wealthy socialite and huge benefactor to the Jewish Children's Bureau of Cleveland. He calls her Aunt Winnie. Rita and Jack are getting married. Gerdy will not let me go. "We don't have money for that," she says. Rita and Susi buy my plane ticket and my new blue-and-white-striped velveteen dress.

A lifelong Zionist and Winnie's best friend, Rabbi Abba Hillel Silver of Temple Tifereth-Israel in Cleveland will perform the ceremony. Aunt Winnie has paid for everything.

Jack wears his Air Force uniform. Rita wears a rhinestone-encrusted tiara with a long lace veil. Her white satin wedding dress has a wide scooped neck with short bell-shaped sleeves. The skirt is covered with yards and yards of white tulle that fall from her slender waist. Rita is radiant. She is beaming with happiness. She looks like a fairy princess.

The band is playing, people are dancing, and I am sitting on Aunt Winnie's lap pleading to her, "Please be my mommy!" I am twelve years old.

CHAPTER FIVE

LOVE AND LOSS

The building where I live with Daddy Sam and Aunt Gerdy is only six stories high. The basement is where I do the laundry. The lobby has stained-glass windows. A large smoked mirror covers the wall. The ceiling has beige-colored antique molding and a large chandelier. The entrance is a heavy glass door covered in fancy iron grillwork. The marble floor is where I teach myself how to roller-skate.

I don't remember the first time I notice the tall, sturdy black man leaning against the basement stairwell of my apartment building. I learn he is Joe the super. He talks to me whenever he comes to fix something in the apartment. Occasionally, I see him walking, holding the hand of a little girl, his daughter Ellen. Along with the duty of cleaning up the kitchen after dinner, it's my job to take the garbage down to the basement. In the winter I use the elevator, but in the summer I walk down the courtyard steps. The basement is where Joe and Ellen live in a single dark and dingy room.

Ellen is short and chubby and a year younger than me. She has a round, happy face with thick, knotty hair that she teaches me how to braid. I learn to play hopscotch. Even though she is better at it than I am, she is never impatient with me if I can't pick up the pebbles. Sometimes Joe comes to watch us, holding a glass of milk and a treat in his hands. Ellen and I always drink from the same glass and take bites from each other's special treat. I eat with them even if I have already eaten, or if I am soon going to eat. They feel like family.

I love Joe and his daughter. Ellen has no mommy either. She and I love to eat. She gives me her special lunchbox, the one with the picture of a puppy on it. She makes me laugh. She teaches me how to play hopscotch and braid hair. She loves me.

One evening, having been smacked in the face by Aunt Gerdy several times for talking back—about what I don't remember—I tearfully clean the kitchen, pick up the garbage, and go to the basement. I pray I will not see Joe or Ellen. I don't want to play; I cannot eat or smile. As I am putting the garbage bag in the big can, I see a stray cat. She is dirty and crying. Thinking she must be hungry, I rush upstairs and sneak into the kitchen for a bowl of milk. I hurry back downstairs and am glad to see the cat still there. I set the bowl down, but when I try and pick her up, she scratches me. When I cry out, Joe asks to look at my scratched arm. He rushes to his room and comes back holding a piece of cotton and a bottle of peroxide. He cleans my wound and wipes away my tears. Then he notices the handprint on my cheek. He wraps his arms around me and holds me close. I can smell the grease and dirt of his overalls as he strokes the back of my head. I want to stay in his arms forever, but I know I have to get back. I kiss his cheek and thank him for taking care of me.

As I walk away, I hear him say, "Honey, don't you forget, you is God's little angel."

It is Ellen's eleventh birthday when Joe surprises her with a chocolate-vanilla iced cupcake (our favorite) with one thick candle in the middle. We are singing "Happy Birthday" in their dark, windowless, one-room apartment, which is now filled with light and laughter, when suddenly Aunt Gerdy appears. With a polite half smile she looks at Joe and tells him that I have chores to do and that it is time for me to leave.

As we walk in silence back to the apartment, she looks coldly at me and says, "I don't ever want to see you with those *Schwartzes* again." I have never heard this German word before, yet somehow I know it is something bad.

I throw away the lunchbox and stop playing hopscotch.

CHAPTER SIX

CASTAWAY

I am in the seventh grade. The class show is about freedom and America. I will play the Statue of Liberty, the most important part, and sing the words of the poet Emma Lazarus that are inscribed on the statue's base. My dress is made from an old white sheet that the teacher drapes over my shoulder. My crown is made from tinfoil glued onto cardboard, and my torch is constructed out of painted papier-mâché. The play will be performed in the large auditorium because not only will it be seen by the whole student body, but by the parents as well.

Our history teacher, Mrs. Theodore, helps us write the invitation, which lists the cast and instructs our parents to sit in their assigned seats in the first two rows. I proudly hand the invitation to Aunt Gerdy. Daddy Sam will have to work and cannot be there. Rehearsal goes on for months, but I memorize all my lines in the first week. As the time approaches, I am so excited to play that great lady that I can hardly sleep. I remember standing on the deck of the ship when I arrived five years earlier and hearing the loud shouts on board: "Look! The Freedom Lady!" It will be a thrilling moment to sing those beautiful words loud and clear: "Give me your tired, your poor, your huddled masses yearning to breathe free!"

The music begins as we march to our places on the stage. The lights go down and the spotlight shines on me, the Statue of Liberty. I see my other teacher, who is sweet and kind and so different from Mrs. Lynch. She is in the wings behind the curtain, looking proudly at me as I sing my song. There is thunderous applause. I am dizzy with happiness.

The lights go on, I take my bow and, blinking back tears, I see that Aunt Gerdy is not there.

Aunt Gerdy would rather stay home and listen to the ballgame.

* * *

Several months later, the school principal, Mr. Vaughn, announces that there will be a school talent show in the auditorium. A talent scout will be in the audience to award a prize to the winners.

I have been going to Estelle Field's dance studio in the front of her ground floor apartment in the building with a curved entryway. The price is right, only a dollar or two. It gives Aunt Gerdy a free hour because she makes me drag my eight-year-old cousin Michel with me to class. He just sits on the floor and watches. I hate class. I am only four feet, five inches tall and weigh eighty pounds. I am chubby and clumsy and embarrassed by my body.

But what I love and am really good at is singing. I quickly sign up in the talent show's singing category. We all have a month to practice. I am told I can sing any song I want and must bring my own sheet music for the piano player. I will sing "I Wonder Who's Kissing Her Now," a song I have loved ever since I first heard it in 1947, the year after I arrived.

I am determined to win the contest. I memorize the melody immediately, but need more time to memorize the lyrics. I practice the pose I will use when I sing the song, looking at myself in the oval mirror of the black vanity in Daddy Sam and Gerdy's bedroom. I realize I need a much larger mirror. Gerdy is lying on the sofa listening to the baseball game and when she asks where I am going, I lie and say that I am going upstairs to Barbara's house. With the sheet music hidden under my blouse, I walk to the lobby and stand in front of the big cracked mirror. First I try looking coy by tilting my head to the left while I sing, but I am not happy with that look. Now, I copy the look of the beautiful movie stars in the magazines that I secretly look through when Gerdy sends me to the store for her Kent cigarettes. I part my lips and smile just a little and tilt my head to the right.

Still not satisfied with those poses, I look straight ahead and, holding my arms very still at my sides, I decide that every time I sing the word "I," my hand will go to my chest to show that I am singing about me.

I wear my brown corduroy skirt over the crinoline, which I soaked in sugar water to make it really stiff. It will hide my fat. I pinch my cheeks, press down on my lips to make them red, and walk to center stage. Handing my sheet music to the piano player, I see that the auditorium is full. Once again, Aunt Gerdy is not here. I open my mouth, begin to sing, and forget the words. I look over at the piano player and feel that surely everyone is going to start laughing. With a reassuring smile, he moves his lips to the words of the first line and starts to play. I place my arms at my sides, put a big smile on my face, tilt my head, and clearly sing out, "I Wonder Who's Kissing Her Now."

And as I have rehearsed, every time I sing "I," my hand goes to my chest. The audience loves all of it! And I love them! I wish the magic would last forever.

The talent scout announces, "The winner is Sylvia Goodman!" I feel like a star. The prize is a series of singing lessons, with the possibility of a recording contract. I am told that the scout will come to my home later to get permission from my parents.

When the scout arrives, Gerdy invites him to have a seat in the living room so they can talk. He speaks at length about my beautiful voice and how with some training and guidance, I have the potential to develop into a serious singer. Gerdy looks pleased and surprisingly interested at this news until he mentions that there will be a slight cost. I have really only won one free lesson, he says, and I will get the rest at a special discounted price. Having lost interest and patience, Gerdy stands up. "We can't afford that, but thank you for stopping by. Let me see you to the door." I stop singing.

* * *

April 8, 1952. A very important day, because my Daddy Sam takes off from work, I take off from school, and together with Aunt Gerdy we go downtown. Today, the judge will change my name from Goodman to Kleinman, and make me Aunt Gerdy's real child. Now she will hug and kiss me just like she does Michel and Stuart. She will finally say how much she loves and wants me. She won't scream or smack me with hands that have a life of their own and always land on my face and head, whether we are walking down the street or in a store or at home. In my naïve, thirteen-year-old heart, I believe that she doesn't show me affection because I am not really hers. Things will be different now. I won't have to clean, cook, and iron to show I am a good girl. I can stop remembering Rita's early warning and I won't need to be afraid that Aunt Gerdy will order me to get out. The good enough me will finally be allowed entry. I am ready and eager to swear my allegiance to a new mommy. I picture her walking down the street, holding my hand, and with pride and joy introducing me as her daughter.

The adoption does not take long, maybe a half hour in the judge's chamber. There are lots of papers to be signed and everyone is rather solemn and formal. We all shake hands in congratulations, politely smile as we leave, get on the subway, and go home. Daddy changes his clothes, gives me a hug and a kiss on the cheek, and goes to work.

Gerdy hands me the broom.

CHAPTER SEVEN

TANGO

In the summer of 1954, Sam and Gerdy rent a large wooden house in the town of Fleischmanns, New York, in the Jewish Catskills. The house has a big eat-in kitchen with windows that look out onto a wraparound porch. We share the house with the May, Herman, and Jacob families who are friends from Washington Heights and who, like Gerdy and Daddy, are refugees from Nazi Germany. The women and children stay in the house all summer while the men, who work all week, come on the weekends. The large kitchen is where the women play cards, cook, preserve freshly picked berries, smoke, eat, and talk. The smell of apricot dumplings, steaming fresh blackberries for jam, and brisket with potato pancakes lingers for days.

Although I am slow to learn most of the lessons at school, I quickly learn the lessons of summer in Fleischmanns. I learn how to pick blackberries, blueberries, and strawberries. I learn that I love big wraparound wooden porches and walking barefoot on the grass. I learn how to bowl and play Monopoly. I learn to ride a bike and to row a boat on Lake Switzerland. I discover the jukebox and play my favorite tunes over and over again. I learn how to flirt, how to play spin the bottle, and how to kiss. Finally I have found something I am really good at.

The summer I meet Rudy in Fleischmanns, I am fifteen and he is nineteen. He is working his way through college as a waiter at the famously upscale St. Regis Hotel. I imagine him to be my long-awaited Prince Charming who will rescue me from my loneliness. He has an easy smile, a twinkle in his eyes, and a handsome, brooding face. He is Hungarian and, although he won't tell me how he survived, I know he is a child of the Holocaust too.

I am five feet tall and weigh 150 pounds. Rudy is the first person to look far beyond my fat body. When he looks at me, he does not see the failure I believe I have become. He does not treat our friendship lightly and never lets on that he knows I have a really big crush on him. He makes me feel that what I have to say is important, and that I am pretty and fun to be with. He enjoys our times together and seeks me out.

We see each other every night after he finishes work, meeting at Fanny's, the local village hangout. Fanny's has a large soda counter with stools in the front, while the back room is filled with tables and chairs, a small dance floor, and a shiny jukebox. The Lindy is the rage, and Rudy and I dance the night away. But on this one special night, when he leads me to the dance floor, he whispers that he will teach me how to dance the tango. I am embarrassed about being short and fat and afraid that I look clumsy with two left feet, but Rudy only holds me tighter, calming my fears. "Just relax, look at my face, follow me, I will lead you," he says. He is a patient, skilled leader, and soon it feels as if I have danced the tango all my life. Rudy whirls me around the dance floor, and always ends by dipping me. With eyes closed I pray that my body will not betray me and that I will not fall. Even when he is sitting with his buddies, as soon as he hears the familiar refrain of Leroy Anderson's "Blue Tango" playing on the jukebox, he walks over to my table wearing a big smile and escorts me onto the dance floor.

I adore him. Because we were not born in America, we both feel like we are living among people who could not fathom what we have been through and what we have lost—our family, our language, and our home. We know that being different is not a good thing, but we know each other's secrets and histories and we are comfortable with each other. Rudy is a young, old man—gentle, smart, sad, and, like me, wants desperately to fit in. He has an old-world charm, and he's determined to make something of himself.

The women are busy cleaning the house before we all go home. The men are loading their cars. I run quickly to Fanny's to tell Rudy that I am going home. We had talked about seeing each other in the city. "We'll go to a movie," he'd said. "Where's Rudy?" I ask his friends. "Oh, he left. School starts early this year." I throw away the small lined paper on which I had scribbled the Kleinmans' telephone number.

CHAPTER EIGHT

NO MORE TEACHERS
NO MORE BOOKS

In 1955, the envelope from Germany comes addressed to me. It is the first time Gerdy gives me my mail unopened. The German document, which I ask Gerdy to read, tells me that the enclosed check in the amount of 6,000DM (less than US $1,500) is my share of the 18,000DM German-government payment for the murder of my parents. What a shock; this is the first time in the last ten years that Gerdy has allowed the names of my parents, especially my mother's, to be spoken aloud in this house. It seems that Gerdy had initiated a claim in 1953 on behalf of my two sisters and me with the help of a German lawyer whose office is down the street from my daddy's fur salon. "Now I can replace this old living room couch," she demands. "And whatever is left is yours."

The new living room couch cost $300, and despite my resentment that I have to pay for my freedom, I am happy knowing that finally I have found my way out.

I think back to my early school years. They were filled with tears, fears, and negotiations. I felt overwhelmed with the need to navigate my way through the maze of confusion and the demands of Aunt Gerdy.

"Learn English!" "Learn math!" "Learn to fit in and act your age, fast!"

But I'm only eight! I'm only nine! I'm only ten! Please be patient with me, I want to scream out. *Tell me, how do all these ages act and speak?*

Now that I am sixteen, school has become unbearable. Math is harder to follow than ever before. French, my foreign language, might as well be Russian. I cannot grasp any of it. Nothing of my childhood French comes back to me; it does not even sound vaguely familiar. The only way to graduate, I am told, will be to go for a secretarial degree. That means I will have to complete Stenography 1 and 2, and, of course, be able to type forty words per minute. I will not graduate at all, for I can only type ten words a minute. I barely pass Steno 1 and I know that passing Steno 2 will be an impossible feat.

"I am quitting high school," I tell Gerdy in my junior year, hoping she will approve. "I want to learn to be a hairdresser like Rita. I will pay for hairdressing school with the money from Germany." I tell her that after graduation, the school will find me a job. I know I will have no problem getting Gerdy to agree after I promise, "I will give you money every week."

It is so exciting to enter the subway in Washington Heights, wearing my white uniform and carrying my small school case that holds my scissors, rollers, clips, and the other tools of my new trade. It is exciting to travel alone to Wilfred Academy on Broadway and 52nd Street. It feels like I have been released from prison and that I am someone else in a whole new life. Now I am a grown-up. Gerdy cannot hit me or tell me what to do. School is easy now. I love learning how to cut, curl, and color hair. For the first three months we practice on heads made of muslin with fake hair. The last three months we work on actual clients. I am already a pro. My fingers dance on hair as I style and cut. I know that I am really good and will have no trouble landing a job in the finest Fifth Avenue salon.

Gerdy volunteers to be my model for all the many contests I enter and win in finger waving and hairstyling. She loves the attention of the crowd that always surrounds us. I'm really good at styling and cutting hair, but when I practice hair coloring her hair ends up being yellow, orange, or with a slightly greenish tint. Gerdy shows unusual patience when she has to wear a scarf for days as she waits until one of the teachers has time to correct my mistakes.

Every Friday my new friends from class and some of the female teachers go out to eat. We talk about who we are, our lives outside of school, and how eager we are to make lots of money so we can be somebody.

I never tell them about my early life, or where I have come from, or what I have lost.

CHAPTER NINE

DOOMED

I am with my new friends in a popular dance hall in the heavily German neighborhood of Yorkville when I meet Mr. Seville. I am seventeen and he is twenty-five. Maybe this handsome Spanish man will be the one Rudy could not be—the hoped-for prince. I love his dark good looks. He makes me feel beautiful.

I am a high school dropout enrolled in hairdressing school, spending the summer home alone while the whole family is vacationing in Fleischmanns for a month. I don't remember the music and I don't remember the dance. All I remember is his arms and how good I feel being held. It starts with romantic dinners in cheap, dimly lit, authentic Spanish restaurants. During dinner, the room becomes still, the waiters disappear, and the gypsy woman accompanied by her guitarist begins to sing in a voice that sounds like a long moan. Suddenly a handsome, sexy man is clapping his hands together above his head and a beautiful black-haired woman with castanets meets him in the center of the room. Clicking their heels on the wooden floor, they dance to the song of the gypsy woman.

Breathless, I watch their dance of fiery passion, jealousy, torment, desire, and sex. Nuzzling me and whispering his soft, Spanish-accented words in my ear, Mr. Seville translates the language of the flamenco. "This, my beauty, is the language of love and life." We spend every evening together, and three weeks later he promises me his devotion and love if only we can become more intimate. He promises that sleeping with him will not only give new meaning to our relationship but it will also make me a real woman. He swears that if I surrender my virginity, he will never treat my gift lightly. He will make me his forever.

Summer is coming to an end, the Kleinmans are coming home, and I know the flamenco will soon be over. All I know about sex is from the *Modern Romance* magazines that I read and keep hidden under my bed. They tell me about romantic love and happily ever after. Man meets salesgirl, or waitress, or airline stewardess, or stranger in the elevator. She's single, or married and unhappy, a young widow, or divorced and struggling. It's never easy for the couple. There is always a jealous friend, boyfriend, parent, or child. All ends well in the end. They live in a lovely suburban house with window boxes of red geraniums and a white picket fence. Sex for me is being held in Mr. Seville's arms. I will be safe and loved and cherished forever. I will finally belong. I will never be alone again.

Two days later, I leave school early, hurry home, shower, apply perfumed body lotion, and put on the sexy new underwear I bought just for him. I pay special attention to my face, hoping that if my hazel eyes are lined and my lashes mascaraed, my cheeks softly blushed, and my lips lined with rose-colored pencil, he will not notice my rolls of fat, my wide hips, and my large behind. He registers us as man and wife in a small, old hotel somewhere on 14th Street in downtown Manhattan. Holding my hot and sweaty hand, Mr. Seville leads me down a urine-smelling hallway with a stained and frayed carpet to our dark, putrid-smelling room. I have made a terrible mistake. Sensing my doubt, Mr. Seville takes me in his arms and presses my face to his chest and reassures me that he loves me. Now I will belong fully, only to him.

I ask him to turn off all the lights. Despite the care and time I took to make up my face, I do not want him to see my five-foot-two, 150-pound body as I undress. In the dark, I lie down on the bed and close my eyes. Not knowing what to do, I wait for Mr. Seville to make a real woman out of me. I am shocked at the feel and weight of his naked body. My submission quickly turns to fear as I struggle to get up. He is rough as he holds both my arms down over my head and, in a voice that has gone from being sweet and gentle to loud and angry, he demands that I lie still. I begin to cry and beg him to let me dress and leave. He takes less than a minute.

I feel a burning pain as I walk slowly to the bathroom and turn on the light. I look in the mirror, expecting my eyes to show the real woman he promised I would become: a woman radiating confidence and glowing with happiness. Instead I see eyes full of sorrow and shame. What have I done?

He does not call.

Three months later, I discover that I am pregnant. What will I do? Where can I go? I cannot burden Daddy Sam with my shameful secret. This kind, gentle man, who always lay awake at night until I was safely home, who kissed me good night no matter how late or how tired he was, who carried me in his arms to the emergency room when a rusty nail lodged itself in the sole of my foot, and cried the one and only time that he was told to hit me—for lying to Gerdy about something—is now, at age thirty-seven, a changed man. He cannot play soccer. He walks with difficulty and drags his leg. His speech is slurred, making him agitated and unable to concentrate. I miss our alone times and want to recapture them, but he shows little interest in doing that now. I see that he is much too worried and frightened about what this sudden, unfamiliar, crippling illness is doing to his mind and body. He has only enough space for himself now. Just when I most need his unconditional love, this strange new affliction has made him unavailable to me.

Because Daddy Sam can no longer take public transportation to work, Gerdy is forced to learn how to drive and to buy a car. In the end, Gerdy will spend three years driving him all over Manhattan and Queens to witch doctors who give him vitamin shots, amphetamine shots, steroid injections, bogus expensive treatments, useless medicines, and false hope. But his symptoms only keep getting worse until he is forty-one, when a real doctor finally diagnoses him with multiple sclerosis.

I can no longer close my skirt buttons, so I must tell Gerdy that I am pregnant. She does not yell. She does not hit me— although I almost wish she would. The smacks, the fists, the wooden spoon, the screaming did not hurt as much as Gerdy's tone of disgust and look of indifference, when she says, "You ungrateful, selfish girl. You're just like your sister Susi. She was sixteen, too, when she met that *goy* in hairdressing school who got her pregnant. She even had the nerve to ask us to meet her husband and that baby. I warned her that she better stay away. Sam was so afraid you would end up like her. He loves you. He wanted to avoid that for you. That's why I agreed to the adoption—and this is the thanks we get."

She does not ask who the man was or whether it had been my first time. All she asks is that I never tell anyone.

Dottie is Daddy's client and friend. She is often in the fur salon when I visit, being fitted for a new coat or sharing her lunch with him. She is vivacious, elegant, and the most beautiful black woman I have ever seen. Abortion is illegal in 1956, but with Dottie's help, Gerdy arranges an abortion for me. Early one morning she drives me in silence to a small building in Harlem. She waits in the car while I enter the dark building where loose garbage is thrown everywhere. Waiting at the top of the stairs, wearing a wide smile and a food-stained apron, is the "nurse." She leads me into the kitchen, where I am told to remove my skirt and underpants and to lie on a worn, stained muslin sheet that covers a wobbly aluminum table. I am not told what will be done, how it will be done, how long it will take, or how much it will hurt.

It looks like a wire hanger that I get back from the cleaners. This is how she will scrape the baby out. Ten teeth-clenching minutes go by before she shouts, "This isn't working! Get dressed right now." She wipes her hands on the back of her housedress and gives me a large black pill. "Take it as soon as you get home," she orders.

"You were much quieter than my other seventeen-year-olds," she says as I put $200 of my money from Germany in her outstretched hand.

Gerdy does not look at me when she drives me home in stony silence. I take the pill, go to bed, and wait. The cramps come every few hours all through the night. In the morning when I use the toilet, I hear the plop. I see a small glob floating in the bloody water. It looks like a piece of liver. My baby! I take a bath, eat some breakfast, change my sweat-soaked sheet, cry with relief, and go to sleep.

I am consumed with shame. I feel old and soiled. I fear that the wire hanger may have damaged me and that I will never have another baby.

Life is hopeless. My secret lies heavy in me and food becomes my only comfort. I eat to fill the sorrow and shame. I am seventeen years old and weigh 180 pounds.

I feel invisible. Now no one can see me.

CHAPTER TEN

SOMEDAY MY PRINCE WILL COME

It is 1958. I am nineteen and living at home, working as a hairdresser at Ila's Salon in the elegant Hyde Park Hotel on Madison Avenue and 77th Street. I share the bedroom with the Humpty Dumpty-covered linoleum floor with my thirteen-year-old brother Stuart. I sleep in a new bed that I buy, not the hand-me-down of my early years. Michel, now fourteen, is allowed to leave school and travel alone to dance in the London production of *West Side Story*, the Jerome Robbins adaptation of Shakespeare's *Romeo and Juliet*, while I am trapped at home.

"The production's single virtue is undeniable and irresistible—it translates its subject into action, in the literal sense of the word. Its theatrical substance is realized not so much in talked plot but in moving bodies," writes John Martin, the dance editor of *The New York Times*.

Gerdy reads this article to us with so much awe and pride. Gerdy gives me none of that admiration or thanks for the money I hand over every week from my hairdressing job, or the bathroom that I clean, or the laundry that I wash and iron, or the meals that I cook. My life is lonely, boring, and hopeless. I worship, adore, and revere Michel. I am consumed with jealousy. It is confusing and painful to feel like this because my love for him is as fierce and deep as my envy.

When Michel comes home two years later he has changed his name to Michel Stuart. I am thrilled and honored that my brother Michel—Gerdy's favorite, worshipped child—trusts *me* with his secret to never tell his mom that not only did he have his first sexual experience with Billy W. (who played a Shark in the show), but that Billy has also turned him on to marijuana.

One year later, I watch Gerdy on her knees, helping Daddy Sam walk. He is forty-four now and shaking and gripping his walker. Gerdy lifts one of his feet in front of the other but his legs are stiff, unwilling, and unable to move without her help. I do not offer to help her. Selfishly, all I care about is rushing out to meet my new Israeli boyfriend, Freddy, at the Middle Eastern café on 92nd Street, where we'd met eight months earlier.

Freddy is not my usual type. I prefer a tall man with a trim waist and dark, wavy hair. My ideal man has black eyes and long lashes; he dresses beautifully, has strong hands and luscious lips, and oozes sexuality and romance.

Freddy has sandy-colored hair, blue eyes, an average build, thin lips, and small hands with fingers that are cigarette-stained. He dresses in jeans and polo-style shirts with the collar turned up. He is the owner of the gas station where he once was hired to do car repairs. It is two blocks away from where he lives with his widowed Russian mother in Washington Heights.

We are in love. I know that this twenty-seven-year-old former Israeli seaman is my long-awaited prince. Three nights a week I wait with Freddy's mother for him to come home from work. As soon as Freddy opens the door she rushes to the stove to heat his food. Without a word Freddy rushes past her and takes me in his arms. "I have to shower and change," he whispers as he walks away. His mother turns off the stove and sits back down. I want to cry. I feel terrible for her. Poor woman, I think. I wish I could say something comforting, but I don't speak Russian. So we sit in silence at the kitchen table, not daring to look in each other's sad, sad eyes.

And, because we have no place where we can be alone, Freddy and I park his car on the corner of a dark, quiet street on Riverside Drive and 125th Street. On the back seat of his shiny red 1953 Studebaker, I lay scrunched up with Freddy fully clothed on top of me. Only his zipper is open with his member ready to enter me.

PART II
Aftermath

CHAPTER ELEVEN

DAMAGE CONTROL

I am twenty-one when I finally move out of the Kleinmans'
apartment. I think I have been planning my escape since the
day that Gerdy threw away my doll when I was eight. I promise
Gerdy that I will come every Friday night to style her hair. I
move in with my friend Eileen, the young colorist at Ila's Beauty
Salon who turned my mousy brown hair Marilyn Monroe
blond. Our new apartment is a cockroach-infested, third-floor
walkup, a railroad flat on the Upper East Side.

"Why couldn't you wait?" Freddy asks. Oh no. Not again.
We have cried and fought about this all year. No answer I
give seems to satisfy him. He cannot make peace with my lost
virginity. "I told you, it was a mistake. I was lonely and naïve."
Sometimes this answer is enough. Sometimes it's not. I cannot
grow my cherry back. This is an ongoing battle that I cannot
win. Will he leave? Will he stay?

In the girlish fantasies I had for my future I always saw myself
with a baby. My early love of mothering that beautiful doll that
Aunt Gerdy threw away has matured into wanting a child of my
own. It is always one child and it always remains a baby.

I am twenty-three and I am pregnant again. Abortion is still
illegal in 1962, so I have Freddy drive me to a clean and sterile

office in Pennsylvania. My favorite client at Ila's salon is a high-class prostitute. When I tell her I am pregnant she gives me the name and address of the kind, compassionate gynecologist and his wife/nurse who perform my abortion.

I hate myself. We drive back to New York in silence. Freddy does not offer nor do I ask him to come upstairs with me. I feel old and soiled. I walk to the bathroom and open the medicine cabinet, where I reach for the aspirin bottle. I just want to sleep and forget what I have done again. Why am I still so naïve and careless? I have to wonder. Did I think that Freddy would overlook my non-virgin state and marry me? Or do I just want a baby? A baby will love me. A baby won't leave me. With a baby I will finally belong. I won't be lonely anymore. That's how the stories in the *Modern Romance* magazines of my childhood always end. It's a smiling, rosy-cheeked baby in Mommy's arms with a handsome daddy looking on. We all live happily ever after.

"Odessa!" I am crying into the phone an hour later to my friend, the black woman who is in charge of the coatroom at Ila's. "I swallowed a bottle of aspirins. Please help me!"

Odessa brings me to the Lenox Hill Hospital's emergency room where they pump my stomach of the hundred aspirins I have swallowed. When I awake, the young intern stands at the end of my bed and, with a look of contempt, tells me to get dressed. "We need the bed for people who are sick and not selfish like you."

This ends my three-year relationship with Freddy. I had believed he was my happily-ever-after. But because I was not a virgin, he believed that I was only good enough to sleep with but not good enough to marry.

CHAPTER TWELVE

MEMORY KEEPER

Gerdy is right. She had predicted, after that pregnancy when I was just an innocent girl of seventeen, that I would never amount to anything. And so I haven't. I am stupid and worthless, alone and filled with self-loathing. There are days that instead of going to my hairdresser job, I stay curled up on my bed in an unwashed sweatshirt eating bologna sandwiches and Drake's chocolate-covered peanut butter cakes. I am unraveling.

I call my sister. I am in need of care and love. Only Rita can exile the voices in my head, a dark swamp of self-loathing. "You just come home to me," she says in her soft, German-accented voice. Ten hours later my cousin Herbert, Papa's sister Edith's son, will drive all night from Cleveland, where he and Rita live. He will ring the downstairs buzzer to my apartment with strict orders from my sister that he not leave the city without me. He will drag my half-empty suitcase and me into the car, with me screaming, "I can't leave New York! I don't want to go!" as he drives me home to her.

Nine hours later we are in the driveway of Rita's home in Cleveland. Rita smiles with her whole body and her hazel eyes sparkle when she sees me. Her arms are open and ready to embrace me, the "baby." A steaming pot of her freshly made chicken soup is waiting to give me instant comfort and relief.

Rita and I are sitting in her Cleveland kitchen. While she bites into a thick slice of German salami and a big-bulb, raw green onion, she begins to tell the story—my story—of the early life that I do not remember.

"There was a lady who took us to a Catholic orphanage in Annecy, France, after Mama and Papa were deported and we had been smuggled out of the camp at Rivesaltes. The nuns were hiding Jewish children. But one night the SS came knocking on the door and told the old sister that they'd learned she was hiding Jews. The kind sister answered, 'my children are God's children. They are sleeping and you must come back in the morning.' Sylvia, it was some kind of miracle when the Nazi soldiers left and promised to come back in the morning. The sister summoned the lady again, and she came for us that evening and smuggled us to a safe house in Annemasse, a small French village on the border of Geneva, Switzerland."

The smell of the onion is making me nauseous. I cannot concentrate. Maybe salami and raw onion are comfort food for Rita as she shares her bitter, sad memories with me, but still I ask her to please throw the onion away.

"We were taken by three men dressed as farmers, milk cans hanging from their shoulders. They told us to call them 'Papa' in case we were seen and stopped on the way. The men just left us alone at the Swiss border. A bright light came on and a man shouted from the small guardhouse, 'Who goes there?' I said. 'We want to go to our aunt. She lives in Zurich.'

"Then the man in the guardhouse came out and when he looked at you, burning up with fever, he quickly called for the ambulance that took you to the hospital. You stayed there for six months suffering with diphtheria. After that you were sent to a sanatorium for six months. Susi and I never saw you. We were not allowed to visit you. You were four years old."

I am a total stranger to my younger self. The first seven years are a blank slate. I always find it is so hard to really own that life. It's always Rita's version. I'm left wondering. Is that true? Was I really like that?

There is not a single moment when I can tell Rita, "Oh yes, Rita, I remember how frightened I was!" I remember nothing.

CHAPTER THIRTEEN

MY BABY BOY

I am twenty-six when I meet a handsome, silver-haired, olive-skinned stranger who coos, "What a cute dog!" when I walk my nine-year-old Yorkshire terrier Fauntleroy. I call him Faunt; he is a gift from my brother Michel.

"I'm worried about you," Rita says on the phone. "What's wrong with you, Sylvia? You need to settle down. Have a family. You have to stop bouncing around like this. You're so pretty and smart. Why can't you find a man?"

My sister sees a marriage license and a wedding band as talismans that will keep me safe from harm. It is a symbol for her that I will finally be taken care of. "That's your happily ever after, honey," she adds.

I really want a child, but it is 1966, and women who do that without being married are called ugly names. So eight days after I meet him, I marry Ben Cataldo, the handsome, forty-three-year-old Italian stranger I met while walking my dog on Mulberry Street in New York's Little Italy.

We move into a large, furnished, one-bedroom apartment in a gorgeous, prewar building in the West Village across the street from my brother Michel. I first meet the black maids, Mabel, Sadie, and Kitty, down in the clean, gray basement room lined with washing machines and ironing boards. Sadie and Mabel work for an elderly couple on the eighth floor. Kitty works for the friendly Judge and his wife who live on the fifth floor. It is Mabel who teaches me how to tuck the corners of a flat sheet tight like she had done when she worked as a hospital aide. It is Sadie who shows me how to fold a fitted sheet by folding the two corners into each other. But it is Kitty who teaches me the power of a smile and a song. I love her right away.

One year later I am pregnant. "Thank you, God!" I crave vanilla shakes, Granny Smith apples, fresh whipped cream with or without the cake, and everything chocolate.

Gerdy has been a waitress in a family-owned restaurant on Wall Street for the last four years. But now that Daddy Sam has sold his business and is confined to a gray La-Z-Boy recliner watching television, she takes over an out-of-business coffee shop near where I grew up. She renovates the shop and turns it into a popular and thriving German-Jewish delicatessen. I visit once or twice a week to eat her homemade tongue, only the center cut—where the fat is—piled high between two slices of fresh, unseeded rye bread, with a side of homemade German potato salad and coleslaw. She always packs me a doggie bag and a sandwich for Daddy Sam, which I bring to him and hold in my hand while he eats.

"This is my daughter Sylvia," Gerdy brags to her customers, pointing to my belly with a joy that I have never seen on her face for me. She shouts, "I'm going to be an oma!"

Ten days later I get a call from my brother Michel, telling me that Gerdy has died of a massive heart attack. She is forty-eight. I am seven months pregnant. Cold currents creep down my neck and vibrate down my arms. Oh God! I'm sorry! I'm sorry for everything I ever said or thought about her! So often I had watched Gerdy on her knees helping Daddy Sam walk, and instead of offering to help, I could not wait to run out of there.

I cannot remember her ever reading to me or holding my hand or leaning down to say something sweet to me when I was young. But she must have, I think. Yet, it is always my Daddy Sam that I remember doing those things. How many times had I wished her dead? And now she was.

Michel places Daddy Sam in the Beth Abraham Nursing Home. Stuart and I pack up the apartment. I am surprised when I find Gerdy's birth certificate and see that when I arrived after the war, she had only been twenty-seven years old and had just given birth to Stuart three months earlier. In spite of living in already cramped conditions, she had agreed to be saddled with a wounded, needy seven-year-old and my fourteen-year-old sister. Despite this added burden, she did not refuse when the husband she adored told her he would bring his murdered sister's children to America.

Her jewelry box is mostly filled with costume jewelry. But there was one ring she never took off, one with real, tiny diamonds lined with even smaller rubies. I tell Stuart to give it to his young wife. Lying under a strand of fake pearls, gold-plated pins, and rings is a shiny, green glass, four-leaf clover pin, which she never wore. I bought it for her with my weekly twenty-five cents allowance when I was twelve years old. Even then I failed to win her love and affection with this pin. When I was older I bought her gifts at Saks Fifth Avenue, Lord and Taylor, and Macy's. Not even those brought the longed-for response. *"Love me, love me" is what they meant.* Buying love began with that four-leaf clover, and that will only end when I begin to love myself, more than forty years later.

I suffer an onslaught of emotion and feel an intense, overwhelming, permeating shame when I read a document that she received just six months before my sisters and I arrived stating that her entire family had also been murdered. What guilt and sorrow she must have suffered, knowing all that her parents had done to buy her way out of Germany.

I don't have any memory of her funeral. I don't know if I was even there. But I must have been and I would have been sobbing with guilt and shame. There was still so much I wanted to say to Aunt Gerdy, so much I hadn't yet said. *"I never felt that you really loved me. I wish you'd been more like a mother to me."* My hope was always that she would apologize, that she would admit how scared or overwhelmed she was back then, and that she would take me in her arms and I would finally feel like her own beloved daughter.

Three weeks later, I sit doubled up in pain in the back of a cab on the way to the hospital, with my husband Ben shouting at the cab driver, "Please go faster! My wife is bleeding!"

I am in my seventh month and my baby weighs only two pounds. My son, whom I name after King David, is born. There is a waiting incubator that will keep my David warm and safe. An intravenous line is stuck in the vein of his tiny arm. On his chest (the size of my palm) are little plastic cups with wires attached to a machine that monitors his heart rate, his breathing, and his temperature. He will be removed from his plastic-covered crib and allowed to go home when his weight reaches five pounds.

Every day I sit by his side and whisper, "Live, my warrior king! Live, David, live." I long to hold and touch him but all I can manage is to squeeze a finger or two through the small opening on the side of the incubator to hold his tiny toe. I fear that because I had refused to let go of my self-pity, and had so often wished her dead, that I am responsible for Gerdy's death. I am twenty-eight years old, yet I cling to this childish notion that God will deem me unworthy of my son, this most precious gift.

As I silently attempt to beg and cut a deal with God, steady tears roll down my face. "Please, God, do not take my little boy! I will give up everything else! I will do whatever you want! I will be whoever you want me to be! Just please, God, don't take my little boy!"

Five weeks later I bundle up my pink-cheeked, five-pound baby boy in my arms and take him home. "Thank you, God!"

CHAPTER FOURTEEN

THE LOONY BIN AND ME

My husband will not make love to me and when I try to arouse him he pushes me away, saying, "We will wake the baby." I am certain that my once-ardent lover must now find me disgustingly fat and undesirable. I will lose the fifty pounds of pregnancy weight.

"Take one pill before breakfast, follow this simple food plan, and see me next week," orders the "diet" doctor. Six weeks later I need more than one pill a day to curb my appetite, so I visit another diet doctor who gives me a new pill that I take three times a day. Three months later the one pill in addition to the three is no longer enough. I add another diet doctor. Soon I am visiting five doctors, and once a month I take my new prescriptions to five different drugstores.

Ben owns a bar and works nights and, because I swallow twenty of those little magic pills a day, I am so wound up that I wash the windows, clean the carpet, and do the laundry all through the night. I'm up, up, up. I cannot sleep. Now I must find a different doctor for pills to bring me down. One early morning I awake from a drug-induced sleep to find a big hole from my cigarette in the pillowcase. I had fallen asleep with it in my mouth. I could have set fire to the house, to me, to my precious baby.

Eight months later, in the middle of the night, with my sweet, eleven-month-old baby sleeping peacefully in his crib, I call my brother Stuart. Newly married and with no money for college, he has taken an entry-level banking job on Wall Street.

"Stuart, I have bugs crawling all over me. Please come!" He finds me naked and bloody. I have tried to carve the imagined bugs out of my skin. I reek of the Lysol that I have used to wash my vagina. I am convinced that I am dirty and smelly and that is why Ben does not want me. I have not slept for seven days and nights. I do not know that from his apartment in Riverdale, Stuart has called St. Vincent's Hospital to tell them that his sister is hallucinating and hysterical, demanding that she and her baby be checked for bug bites, and that they should have a straitjacket ready for her.

"My baby, my baby! Give me my baby!" I scream at the nuns in the hospital who have grabbed my yawning little boy out of my arms. They run down the long hospital hall with me chasing frantically after them, screaming, "Please, that's my baby! Give me my baby." I let out an unrestrained wail that cuts through the air.

* * *

I am wearing a faded, untied hospital robe when I awake on a bare mattress on a stained, cracked linoleum floor in the corner of a long, wide hall, surrounded by a small crowd of women dressed like me. I am waking up to a nightmare. But it is all too real.

Before I can ask them where I am, a mouse scurries danger-ously close to my naked feet.

"That's a mouse!" I scream.

"Honey, we got lots of them here," they answer. A real mouse!

I am in the psychiatric ward at Bellevue Hospital. I have been asleep from the time I arrived three days earlier. Someone shouts, "Time for meds!" so I follow the zombie-like crowd forming a line. "What is this?" I ask the nurse who's handing out the tiny paper cups. She does not answer so I ask again and still she does not respond. Someone jabs their elbow in my side. "Hon, just take the fucking pill," the woman behind me groans.

We are drug addicts, domestic violence victims, unfit mothers, prostitutes, rape victims, and incest survivors. We are dangerous and crazy. This place is bizarre. I have landed on a strange alien planet. The bathroom is huge and open. A row of toilets lines one side with open shower stalls on the other. No walls, no doors, no shower curtains, no privacy, because there's no telling what "we" will do.

I am in the shower and do not hear her approach until I feel something around my neck. "You're mine now," I hear a woman whisper. I later learn that she has used the belt that she ripped off her robe. Frozen with fear, my throat closes when I try to scream. In my head all I hear is, *"I'm a mother, I'm a mother. I don't belong here."* Then I hear someone shout, "Leave her alone and get outta there or I'll break your fucking face." I've been saved! How could Stuart ship me off to a nuthouse? I'm pissed off at Stuart, at myself, and at my distant, unaffectionate, condescending, and emotionally absent husband Ben.

* * *

Every day is the same. I take my meds. I walk the halls and I beg to call Ben, who has not yet come to see me, and still the nurse answers, "No." I know that Ben leaves for work at his bar at four in the afternoon and does not get home until early morning, when he eats his breakfast and goes to sleep. Stuart and his wife can't take my baby because they both work. Where is my baby boy?

It is day seven and another day in "paradise"—as we ladies refer to this hellhole—when I see a familiar figure get off the elevator and walk toward me. I know that walk, slow and careful since her hip surgery. I know that hat; it's the one she wears to church on Sunday. I know and love that smiling face with eyes that twinkle. I run into her arms. "Whatcha doin' in the nuthouse, girl?" asks a laughing Kitty.

"Don't you worry yourself any," Kitty says. "You just get better. David is staying with me and my Bernard." I am so relieved and happy to know that Ben had reached out to her. This seventy-year-old, full-of-life woman, a laundress for the judge in my building, was my first friend when I came as a new bride to the apartment three years earlier. "Thank you, thank you," I shout to Kitty all the way down the length of the corridor until the elevator door closes.

"You wanna get outta here, hon?" asks my favorite hooker after Kitty leaves. She has hair that looks like bright yellow straw with thick black roots. "Just smile," she says. "You is got one bu-teee-ful smile. And look happy." Is this a life lesson? "The damn doctor is gonna ask your name. They is gonna ask you for the damn year and the name of the damn president. Answer dem three stupid questions and you're outta here, hon."

Twelve days later the "doctor" nods his head in approval as I answer the three questions. He hands me a printout of a list of outpatient therapy offices that I promise to call, and three weeks after my arrival, I leave the Bellevue ward and take a subway to the Lenox Arms apartments to pick up my smiling, one-year-old baby boy from Grandma Kitty. I have called her that from that first moment she took my David in her arms and sang to him when I brought him home from the hospital.

CHAPTER FIFTEEN

DR. BOB

I am thirty years old when I sit in a small, sunny office with Bob Triana, the therapist whom I will see three times a week for the next eight years. It is 1969.

I can't remember what I shared in our first sessions, but I'm sure I used most of the fifty-five minutes crying and raging about my husband Ben. Somewhere around the fifteenth or sixteenth session, Bob finally interrupts this pathetic tirade. "Tell me about your childhood." What! Wait a minute. This is dumb. *How can talking about my childhood change Ben?*

"What do you want to know?" I ask a solemn, stone-faced Bob. The minutes pass like hours as I wait for him to tell me what to talk about. Finally a wretched, twenty-year-old memory surfaces, still so alive in me it could have happened only yesterday.

"It was 1950. I was eleven years old. My Aunt Gerdy was yelling and smacking my face in front of school as the kids passing by tried not to stare. She was furious that my teacher had called her in because I was still having trouble keeping up with the class. I felt helpless and embarrassed. I just coiled into myself. The shame came so fast it felt like nausea."

Just the mention of Gerdy's name and I am slumped in a

bath of tears. "Bob, I just never fit in. The silent message Gerdy gave me was not to show my feelings, unless it was gratitude. Anger, or sadness, or discontent was not allowed. I just shrank in her presence. I wished I could become invisible, that way her rage would just pass over me.

Bob is silent and still stone-faced. Why doesn't he say something? Isn't he supposed to give me some insight into what's wrong with Ben? Shouldn't he offer a drop of sympathy for the violence I suffered at Gerdy's hands? But all he says is "Time's up."

In the sessions that follow, I am sobbing or silent, until Bob says, "That's all for today." In perhaps our tenth session I realize that my silence is not getting me anywhere. I better talk. "Gerdy's rages were so unpredictable. A word or a look could just set her off. I lived in fear and vigilance. I was vigilant. I had to be. I never knew when Gerdy would strike. I learned to look for signs of an oncoming attack. I had to keep her calm. That meant never saying no, and never asking for anything. I tried to make as little noise as possible. I learned that in baseball season she eased up."

I'm sobbing uncontrollably now when I see that eager-to-please, young, lonely, brown-haired girl in my mind. "I was so afraid of Gerdy's temper, but not as much as her silence. It was a cruel form of punishment. Especially when she'd say, 'Oh never mind, I'll do it.' I would beg her to please let me clean or cook or iron or do anything really, just not to feel completely invisible. She thought nothing of the embarrassment and shame that I felt when she'd scream or hit me in the street."

"I was just a child," I want to scream at Gerdy. But she's dead and I can't.

I learn that my marriage is merely a duplicate of all my previous romantic relationships. I pick men who are not like my Daddy Sam, who held me with love and kindness, but who are instead like Gerdy. They do not value me. They too are distant and unavailable. I see that I do not let people get close to me because I fear they will leave when they realize what a rage-filled woman I really am.

"Sylvia, you were still too young and hadn't had the life experience to establish your own identity yet," Bob says. "It would have been impossible for you not to accept the terrible image of yourself that your Aunt Gerdy created. And because you have no self-esteem and believe that you are not worthy of love, you keep attracting men into your life that prove that."

To feel like an outsider is a painful psychic wound. I am desperate for validation, acceptance, and love. I am overly accommodating to everyone—even people I don't know or even like; *especially* those I do not like. While I am always available for nurturing, problem-solving, money lending, and advice giving, I carry a deep-rooted fury that seethes beneath the surface of my lovely smile and my all-giving persona.

"My brother Michel is who I want to be!" I whine to Bob a year later. "He has such a glamorous and exciting life!" Once he became a professional dancer he never again spent more than a month or two at home. Michel was nineteen when he met and fell in love with Ron Field, the Tony Award-winning choreographer. It's so ironic that Ron's Aunt Estelle owned the ground-floor dance studio that I left, and where Michel stayed and learned to dance.

Gerdy idolized him, always bragging about his new show or the beautiful gifts and the weekly letters he sent from all those exotic foreign countries where he danced. She was so proud of him.

In our sessions Bob usually wears a solemn expression on his face, but now he is smiling as he points out, "It was so easy for Michel to show his mother all that love. But, only when he was safely thousands of miles or a hundred blocks away." I wonder if the gifts and beautiful letters, signed with "Much love, Michel," were really my brother's way of keeping his overbearing and adoring mother far away.

Another recollection: Michel is seven and eight and nine years old. Gerdy calls from her bedroom, "Michel, help me hook up my bra." My therapy now tells me this was not as innocent as my eleven- and twelve- and thirteen-year-old self thought.

CHAPTER SIXTEEN

HIS MADONNA

It's 1971 and I have regained all the weight—and more—that I had lost on the diet pills two years earlier. I remember how those pills drove me crazy and landed me in a nightmare. And yet I am grateful because I would not be in therapy if not for those demon pills. During a particularly whiny session complaining about how ugly and fat I am, Bob recommends a new program called Weight Watchers. It will take me about ten months of Weight Watchers meetings and weekly weigh-ins— and not cheating with carrot cakes, Italian cheesecakes, pizza, or ice cream sundaes dripping with hot caramel sauce—for me to lose fifty pounds.

I am now a pretty, thirty-three-year-old woman who weighs 125 pounds, but what I see in my mirror is still my ugly 175-pound self.

My husband Ben still does not touch me. I wear my new red, see-through teddy with matching bikini panties, but not even that arouses him. I'm starving. I don't know how to turn him on. I've tried everything, but then I remember what Maureen had shared about her sugar daddy in our Thursday night group. "He can only get it up after he's had at least six glasses of scotch or his other favorite, gin on the rocks. He's so drunk by then he'd fuck King Kong. It pisses me off. It's degrading, but he takes good care of me, and so I stay."

What pissed you off, Maureen, might just get *me* laid, I tell myself. David is sleeping at a friend's house. I have made Ben's favorite meal of homemade lasagna, accompanied by a large bottle of red wine. I take small, slow sips of wine (I don't drink) as I keep filling his glass. When I see that the bottle is almost empty, I excuse myself. I rush to the bedroom and put on my sexy teddy. I lie down on the bed and wait. When Ben walks in I tear off his clothes and push him onto the bed. He does not resist. I take off my teddy and before I can remove the matching bikini panties, Ben pulls the crotch aside and puts his small penis in. In utter silence and in less than a minute he ejaculates, after which he rolls over and sleeps. The scented lotion I had so carefully spread on my breasts, legs, and buttocks has not been noticed; my body has not been stroked or kissed. My lovely lavender-douched vagina could have smelled like rust. It would not have mattered.

One week later, Ben and I sit in the Park Avenue waiting room of Dr. Soichet, my gynecologist. The folds of skin around my vagina are red and raw from my constant scratching. It is so painful now and the reason I finally called for this appointment today. I adore him, as does every woman who sits in his waiting room. His bedside manner is kind and friendly. He is a Jewish-French Santa Claus minus the beard. His blue-gray eyes twinkle like a mischievous little boy's. Dr. Soichet opens his arms and gives me a warm and welcoming embrace. "Sorry you had to wait so long but I had an emergency delivery. Come with me, Cherie, to the examining room." "I'll just wait out here," says Ben. Dr. Soichet was scheduled to deliver my baby, but because I did not go to full term he was on vacation when I delivered. Ben always came with me during the seven months of my pregnancy. I wonder why he doesn't follow me into the examining room today.

Gonorrhea! I have gonorrhea. What is that? I have never heard this word before. I am embarrassed and ashamed. I don't ask a single question. I have already reasoned that it is because I don't lay toilet paper on the seat when I sit down to pee in a public restroom. And I don't always wash my hands after I'm done. I picked something up from those seats.

I look away when Dr. Soichet hands me the white slip. "Have this prescription filled. In two to three weeks the itching and burning will be gone." I look at the floor, at the magazines, anywhere but at him. No hug. No smile. As I walk out the door, I hear him say, "Ben, can I see you in my office, please?"

Five years after starting therapy with Bob in 1969, I finally hear from him why my husband, the once-ardent lover, no longer desires me. "I suspect that Ben's dysfunction is what Freud calls the Madonna-whore complex, where he divides women into two types. The Madonna is pure and good, and the whore is soiled and bad. Sylvia, your husband does not want a lady in public and a whore in the bedroom. He wants you to be a lady in public *and* in the bedroom. He's put you on some kind of Earth-Mother pedestal, and how can he make love to the mother of his child? Of course Ben rejects your overtures. He does not want you to be sexual or aggressive. Those acts of sex are only meant for dirty women."

Now I want Ben dead. How arrogant I am—how ignorant of me—not to have even considered that he might be getting sex elsewhere and bringing gonorrhea home to me?

I would love to feel my hands around his neck as I choke the son of a bitch to death. I want revenge for the years that bastard let me believe I was to blame. He was silent as he watched me blame myself for being too fat and not pretty or sexy enough for him. I rant and rage. But, strangely, after I calm down and let the anger settle, I am not at all depressed. Instead what I really feel is relieved, a little scared, a little excited. I even allow myself to feel pretty and sexy for the first time in my life.

* * *

Daddy Sam lives in the Beth Abraham nursing home on Allerton Avenue in the Bronx. It is an ugly, gray building where every room smells of urine, feces, and Pine-Sol. Daddy Sam does not remember me, yet his eyes always look at me with tenderness. He cannot walk, he does not speak, and he sits motionless all day in a wheelchair, unshaven, and hooked up to a catheter that collects his urine. When I place my smiling baby boy in his lap, he cries and smiles, and when his atrophied fingers cannot bend I help him hold the only grandchild he will ever know. David is just two when we bury my fifty-two-year-old Daddy Sam on a bitterly cold Sunday morning in 1970.

My thoughts wander as I stand by the grave and a memory floods my mind of other Sunday mornings. What I see is a king-size bed: Gerdy lies on the left, Daddy Sam on the right. Two young boys and their ten-year-old sister are lying in the middle, me always close to Daddy, getting tickled. Everyone is laughing. I remember the smell of Limburger cheese from Gerdy's feet and the lingering odor of the gas that my daddy had passed during the night. But most of all, I remember all the love he had shown me so long ago. And, sadly, I also realize that I should not hold on to my childhood anger about Gerdy's inability to show me any outward affection. But that is where my Aunt Gerdy is still lodged in my mind and just won't budge. I cannot forget how she made me sit week after week, year after year, forcing boiled cod and onions on me.

Bob never asks me to talk about my murdered parents, my stolen childhood, or the lost memory of my first seven years. We never talk about the hidden, frightened, and traumatized child I had been then.

I will not understand Dr. Bob's silence until 1985, when I meet with the kind, Viennese-born therapist Herry Teltscher. I discover that therapists like Bob, Freudian analysts trained in the 1960s, were not trained to work with survivors of the Holocaust. "In the aftermath of the Germans' systematic massacre of the Jews, no voice had emerged that spoke of the enormity of what had happened," Herry tells me. "For three decades, the traumatized survivors and guilt-ridden American Jews, who regretted that they had not done more to rescue their brethren, were frozen in silence."

CHAPTER SEVENTEEN

A SMALL SEED
OF GROWTH

"If your son David just tried harder, he could do it," his third-grade teacher is telling me in 1976. "He doesn't do the work. If he just paid attention, he would get it. When I hand out a simple instruction, he just sits there and stares at the paper as if it were a foreign language. When I ask him to read, he reads many words backward; *saw* becomes *was*; *dog* becomes *god*. When I correct him he becomes frustrated and angry. Last week he hit one of my kids. David has a short fuse."

Ben and I bring our son to St. Vincent's Hospital. "David is learning disabled," the doctor tells us. "We've completed a battery of tests and, academically, David scored above average in math. But with this disability, he will have trouble processing sensory information, and this is why David sees, hears, and understands things differently. The words on the blackboard get scrambled and he reads them backwards. If you ask David to go to your bedroom and get your hairbrush and bring it back to you, all he will remember is to go into the bedroom. We are still very new at researching this disorder, but what we have seen is that it is more common in boys, that it is most probably inherited, and that a premature birth might also be a cause."

I am stunned at this onslaught of information. "The brain has an amazing capacity to change, and children respond when they are given the support and encouragement they need," says the doctor. "David is a very lucky boy that you intervened so early. With some very specific teaching techniques and a few simple exercises, we will retrain David's brain."

Tears of relief spike my eyes when I hear that I am not being overprotective and that, as David's teacher had intimated, my son is not lazy or bad.

Ben sits at the edge of his chair, staring at the door. The doctor looks at me and says, "I recommend that we transfer David to our new special ed class, a program that the hospital has implemented. He will be in a class with only ten children, not the thirty-five that he is with now. Mrs. Block is a trained special ed teacher. She will give David the one-on-one attention he needs to experience success and to end this cycle of failure, anger, and shame."

"David is retarded," says Ben as we walk home.

"He is *not* retarded, Ben!" I hiss back. I feel my rage brewing. I want to scream right there in the street. *You stupid jerk! You macho creep! No wonder I can't stand you.* I say nothing.

"I want him gone," I tell Bob in 1976. Today I do not need Bob's approval or his permission. I will not wait until my Thursday session with Bob's therapy group to share that I want a divorce. I will not look at my behavior. I will not dissect my destructive patterns. I will not look for closure or search for meaning. Nor do I care if I am acting out. I don't want to challenge the demons within. I don't want to hear that leaving this silent, frozen marriage will hurt my son. I know that I have no money and no plan. All I know is that I will not let Bob touch my resolve.

"Bob, I want Ben out now!" I demand.

"That's all for today," says Bob, looking at the clock. I stand up and walk to the door, and just as I begin to leave, Bob smiles and wishes me good luck.

I cannot sleep. I awaken at 3 a.m. My head is filled with "what if" scenarios and questions about how I will manage run through my head. I don't quite trust myself. I feel insecure and my goal is getting fuzzy. Fear and doubt have me in their grip. I am depressed and tired and worried about the future, but I use the three hours I have before Ben gets home to practice my morning monologue.

I begin by using a voice that won't reveal how despicable I think he is or how desperate I am to be free. My voice will be calm and sure. I will pretend to be thinking of his happiness, too. My face will not show the contempt I feel for him. I will wait until after he has slept and eaten, and with the sun-drenched background of the living room, I will ask for a divorce.

It is nearly noon when I hear Ben leave our king-size bed where I have lain untouched and unloved for the last six years. He shouts for David to get ready for baseball practice in the park across the street, an excruciatingly painful father-son scene I watch every week from our sixth-floor apartment window. "You clumsy idiot," Ben will invariably shout to him. Every week that I am forced to watch this dreadful interaction, I envision throwing Ben to the ground, punching him until he bleeds, and then choking him to death. I wish that I could scream out that he is a selfish, stupid, and hopeless loser, but I do not want David to see this imagined scene. So I force myself to remain silent, watching my sweet, precious eight-year-old son, the cowed listener.

Ben sat next to me as the kind doctor explained that because our son is learning disabled, it is difficult for him to follow directions. Ben knows that David is hyperactive and that it is hard for him to stand or sit still. He has zero impulse control and is awkward at sports. He is so easily distracted—it could be a dog, a falling leaf, the chirping birds, or the homeless pigeon lady feeding her flock. All this coupled with his poor visual-motor coordination makes it impossible for David to catch or throw a ball. It is a disaster when his father, whom David loves and tries so hard to please, loses patience and belittles him.

I feel my rage bubble over when I remember the story I shared with Bob about Gerdy. How ashamed Gerdy had made me feel, how humiliated and embarrassed as she hit and screamed at me in front of my school with my classmates looking on. How I too had been the cowed, frightened listener. I will not watch this shocking, wretched, tortured scene unfold one more day.

And yet on this gorgeous morning I forget everything I have spent the night practicing. I am fighting for my son and I want no more of Ben's machismo for my boy. Unplanned and unscripted, like a lioness protecting her cub, I march into the bedroom where Ben is getting dressed. David is eating breakfast in the other room, where he cannot hear my disgust. I am hot with fury when I think about Ben's silence as he watched me blame myself for being too fat and ugly and undesirable. And then, with dread and delight in almost equal proportion, I demand, "I want a divorce."

But first I make Ben promise that he will not tell David until I come back from walking the dog. "We will talk to our son together," I explain. "We'll just tell him that Mommy and

Daddy don't love each other anymore. I want us both to assure him that it is not his fault, that he is a good boy, and that he will spend every weekend with you. Ben, it is very important that David know he is not losing you. That you and I will never fall out of love with him. We need to do this for our child. It will not be easy for him. He has to hear from you and me that we will never, ever leave him.

"Ben, do you promise that you won't say anything to David until I come back with the dog?"

"Yes, I'll wait."

"No, Ben, I want you to say 'I promise.'"

"I said I'd wait."

"Ben, I really need to hear you say *I promise.*" I loathe him. And yet I know that Ben loves his son. No matter what Ben thinks of me, he will do this for his child. Still, I have to bite my lip to keep from screaming at him, afraid that David would hear me. "Okay, okay, *I promise.*" Finally. "Why do you want a divorce?" Ben calmly asks. "Aren't you happy?"

I am stunned. I don't know whether to laugh or cry at his bizarre response. Who is this stranger? Can he really be this blind? Does he not know how miserable we are? Although now I think maybe I am the only one who is miserable here. The dog is whining and sitting by the door; he needs to go out.

I feel my heartbeat speed up slightly, the way it always does when I realize too late that maybe I should not have done or said whatever it is that I have just done or said. I rush to the dog. "Hurry up, Porky. Make a pee-pee for Mommy." When I open the apartment door, my heart clenches with fear at the sight of my David standing alone in the darkened alcove, sobbing. "Mommy, why are you making my daddy leave?"

Monster! Ben promised me, but he just could not wait. Rather than stand together and show David that no one was to blame, now I am the bad one who threw his father out. Right now I wish I could just walk into the living room and grab the brass-handled iron poker from the fireplace, walk to the sofa where Ben is sitting with the racing form circling his bets for the day, and shove the poker right through that bastard's heart.

Instead, I rush to my sobbing, heartbroken little boy and fold him into my arms and say over and over again, "I'm so sorry. I'm so sorry."

CHAPTER EIGHTEEN

WAR STORIES

I am a thirty-seven-year-old single mother in unknown terrain, desperately trying to keep it together, to appear all right for the sake of my son. I am juggling three jobs, seven days a week. By allowing David to visit Ben in his New Jersey home on weekends, during holidays, and in the summer months, I do everything possible to make sure that Ben finds no reason to stop seeing his son. I have not asked for alimony. I want only $100 a month in child support. I'd heard too many horror stories from women about their ex-husbands. How the alimony check always came late or not at all. How degrading it felt to have to call every month and beg for the check. How their kind and happy husbands had turned into angry, cruel, monstrous exes. How they lied and hid their money, and sang their poverty songs and refused to pay.

No, no, no. I have no interest in playing this game with Ben. Only last week my best friend sobbed as she told me that her eight-year-old had come home silent and angry after visiting his dad. "Dad called you a lazy bitch," he spat out. "He's tired of paying your rent. He doesn't even live here anymore."

I ask Ben to pay $25 a week for David. After Ben betrayed me and told our son that I had kicked him out, pitting him against me by playing the poor victim, I know I cannot trust him. Yes, it will be hard. Twenty-five dollars a week pays for only one session with David's tutor, but I don't care. I will never be demanding. I will be accommodating and patient. I will pretend to be happy for him when he tells me about his new job. I will do all this to prevent Ben from blaming me as the reason he no longer visits with his son.

My hairdressing license is expired, and to renew it I must go back to school for three months. I don't have the time or the money. I need a job right now. Eight hours a day, I work in an office as a receptionist. Three nights a week I am a waitress in a hamburger joint on Manhattan's Upper West Side. On the weekends, I answer the phone and give out patient information at Doctors Hospital. Although Bob's words ring in my head, "It's the *quality* of time, not the *quantity* of time, that matters," I am still guilt-ridden about the one hour I spend with my son before I leave for my waitress job three times a week. But I need the extra money to pay for David's tutor, who comes three times a week. Ben has married a woman less than half his age who wants children of her own. One year later, Ben stops coming for David and has his telephone number unlisted. He has abandoned his son.

I am left without any child support. Even with three jobs, I don't have the money for summer camp or a nanny when the school year ends. I won't leave David with a teenager, the only caregiver I can afford.

So I call my sister Rita. "No problem," she answers in her soft German-accented voice. "Just bring Baby David (my son is eight, but she still refers to him as Baby David) to Cleveland."

I will stay a week and then leave David with his Aunt Rita for two months so I can go back and work. Rita and I sit at the table in her big Cleveland kitchen. Just Rita and me, eating thick slices of fresh rye bread spread with sweet butter and honey. I never tire of hearing her tell me the stories about our parents and the early years of a life that I do not remember.

Rita begins with this story:

It was 1942 and we were living in one room of the house of Madame Bouhot and her thirteen-year-old daughter Madeleine in the south of France. But one early morning, two gendarmes (French policemen) came for us. Papa was very sick. They looked over at Papa, suffering from asthma and bedridden, so they shouted, "We'll come back for you later."

Papa whispered for Susi to run to the square and to ask the police prefect to help us. But when she got to the square, the Vichy police chief only shrugged his shoulders at Susi and said, "I can do nothing." (The French Vichy government collaborated with the Nazis.)

Papa was pleading from his bed for them not to take his family as the two policemen led us out of the house. You were crying and clinging to Mama, your chubby little arms wrapped around her neck, as we walked to the square where the buses waited for the arrested Jews to board. Despite his illness, Papa had dragged himself down to the square. As we boarded the bus, Mama looked out and saw Papa hiding behind a tree. With her head leaning up in the direction of the family Bouhot house, Mama silently mouthed, "Geh zurück. Geh zurück. Go back. Go back."

I don't know how long we were on that bus before we were hustled onto a train by French police in black uniforms. The windows of the train were covered with black cloth, and Mama was whispering, "Keine Luft. No air."

The train tracks led directly into the camp. We were hungry and tired. They handed us a thin cup of soup made with rotten tomatoes and separated us from Mama. You clung to me as we were marched into the children's barrack, where the three of us slept on lice-infested straw. Soldiers with guns stood guard outside.

Many weeks later Mama came into our barrack and woke us up. She asked Susi and me to get dressed. She helped you get dressed. And then she told us to go outside while she left without us.

The sun was coming up on a very large open concrete square. Mama was standing with a crowd of people in a long line. We walked to another line. Our line was long too, but it was only the children. We stood outside for a long time and I saw that Mama's pale skin was freckled and red from the sun. When they called out her name, Mama looked over at us and shouted from her place in line, "Go back to the barrack, my sweet girls. I will be back soon!"

You ran from the line with your arms outstretched, crying, "Maman, Maman, emmène-moi avec toi! Mama, Mama, take me with you!"

Mama looked over again and told me to take care of the baby. You were only three years old. And then the French guards who were in charge of the camp pushed her onto the waiting cattle car.

I held your hand as Susi and I walked you back to the barrack, and when I turned around to get one last look at Mama, the sliding door of the train had been closed and locked. It was the last time I would see our mama.

Rita is crying uncontrollably now. How cruel. I have not even a glimmer of memory. Not about Rita or Susi or Mama or Papa. It feels as if I wasn't even there. Rita is talking about a stranger. I only came alive on the ship to America when I was seven. Maybe I just fell from the sky.

I hold my sobbing forty-five-year-old sister in my arms and weep with her.

CHAPTER NINETEEN

WE ARE WARRIORS

I need to pay for David's play therapy twice a week with Dr. Conrad, the young, cheerful, Brooklyn-accented former sanitation worker who had been with me in Bob's Thursday night therapy group. This is in addition to the three-times-a-week tutor I also pay. I will work five jobs if I have to.

"I'm sorry I had to ask you to leave work, but I'm having a problem with David," says Mrs. Block, his new special education teacher. "Even though his grades have improved, I'm afraid he is still acting out. He's extremely hyperactive, and his attention span is only seconds long. I need David to be quiet, to sit still, to focus more, and to show more control. His behavior is very disruptive to the class. I want you to consider having David's doctor prescribe Ritalin for him. All my kids are on it."

But I still remember my year with drugs. I have not forgotten the Thorazine pill I was forced to swallow twice a day in Bellevue, a pill so powerful that it left all fifty women on the ward open-mouthed and drooling, in a zombie-like state. Because I am in love with this young boy who needs everything I can give him, whom I will never stop fighting for, I answer, "No."

I don't remember how I found *Why Your Child Is Hyperactive*, a book by Dr. Ben Feingold. I am just glad I did. The diet made sense and there was no other option. I would not let David get drugged. It had to work.

During his long career, Dr. Feingold mainly studied allergies in children. He noticed that the increase of children exhibiting symptoms of hyperactivity seemed to correspond with the increased consumption of various food additives. In 1970 he set out to study this relationship and believed he had found a link. In his book, Dr. Feingold supported his belief that when hyperactive children don't consume foods that contain salicylic acid, synthetic colorings, and artificial flavorings, their behavior improves and they perform better in school. What emerged from his work was the Feingold Diet, which I decide to try on David.

The diet is time-consuming and hard to follow. I must first learn how to identify the various forbidden additives in all their different forms on the labels that I painstakingly read. Not only must I learn the foods that are allowed, but I must also teach David this complicated and difficult new way of life. I gently teach my eight-year-old son how to explain to his classmates that he is on a strict new diet. I give him the words so that he will not become upset or embarrassed when he explains what this diet is for. David already feels different from what he calls his "normal" friends, Eric and Brian, who live in our building. I know that explaining why he can't eat candy or why he has to eat my special homemade meals will be hard, but I really believe it will help him.

A young Legal Aid lawyer, referred to me by the New York Bar Association, helps me take Ben to court. The lawyer collects the $900 for the nine months of unpaid child support that my ex-husband owes me. It will help to pay for the foods that

David needs on his diet: free of artificial coloring and flavors, and difficult to find in 1975.

Five days a week, six times a day, David must sit in the back of the classroom and eat a hardboiled egg, a quarter cup of freshly ground peanut butter, and a banana. The six-hour glucose test that David took showed an abnormal glucose metabolism. His body was less able to handle the sugar intake. It could not maintain a balanced blood sugar, and like other hypoglycemic people, David had low blood sugar. When that happened, David just zoned out. He became aggressive and hyper. He could not sit still. He could not focus. His lively, sparkling hazel eyes looked empty and blank.

I realize that I've never been there for someone else before my son David, so when I see the results of that six-hour glucose test, I am determined to keep him on this diet no matter what. I feel certain that this modified diet will be good for my boy. I had to convince Mrs. Block to allow David to eat in class. When I showed her the test results she understood why he must do this. She became David's ally and advocate. She was very careful to not draw attention to David when he left his seat to go to the back of the room and eat.

Then there is the pizza, the McDonald's food, and the Burger King food that he cannot eat. There are the sleepovers he must refuse because other moms don't cook like me. And there is the class birthday cake and ice cream that he cannot eat and the Coke and Kool-Aid that he cannot drink.

Without his full cooperation, this diet will not work. We start to see the changes immediately. Where before he could not concentrate, sit still, or hold his attention for more than a mere second, David is now more focused and alert. My brave son sees the result of his hard work. He begins to exhibit a real commitment to following the diet, and he has less of a problem saying, "I'm not supposed to eat that."

I fought like a warrior. It was hard to make my eight-year-old son admit that the diet could work. I won the war over the burger and the Coke.

CHAPTER TWENTY

IDENTITY ISSUES

I am sitting with my brother Michel's companion, Tommy Tune, in the Shubert Theatre for the opening of *A Chorus Line*, a new musical from Michael Bennett. It is 1975. For this show Michel is forbidden to reveal any information about it to anyone in advance of opening night. The playbill explains that the concept began on a snowy January night in 1974, in an empty Nickolaus Exercise Center on East 23rd Street. Eighteen Broadway dancers gathered and spent all night talking into a tape recorder about their lives and what drove them to become dancers.

It is a saga of the underappreciated and overlooked. The hustling, high-kicking, barely known hoofers without whom the stars of the show would have no one to dance in front of. These are the dancers who travel from musical to musical, chorus to chorus, but are always in the background.

When the curtain opens, we are at an audition for an upcoming Broadway production. The formidable director Zach (the Michael Bennett character) and his assistant choreographer Larry are putting the gypsies through their paces. Zach tells them he is looking for a strong dancing chorus of four "boys" and four "girls." He wants to learn more about them and asks the dancers to introduce themselves. With some reluctance, the dancers reveal their pasts. The stories are of early life experiences through adulthood.

Stepping downstage, the first candidate, "Mike," opens up as he recalls his first experience with dance, when he was a kid being dragged along to his sister's dance classes, as he sings.

"I'm watching Sis go pitter-pat. I can do that. I can do that. One morning Sis won't go to dance class. I grabbed her shoes and tights and ran seven blocks in nothing flat. I got to class and had it made, and so I stayed the rest of my life. All thanks to Sis, now married and fat. I can do that! I can do that!"

"Tommy!" I whisper. "That's our story! That's Michel and me!"

Through my tears, I see in my memory two little boys who wait in bed for their ten-year-old sister Sylvia to tell them a bedtime story. There is no television and we are not allowed until we are much older to listen to the radio at bedtime. In that dark room, for one hour each night, I transport us into a magical world where little girls are never punished or hit. Mommies love their little girls, the wicked stepmother always dies, the handsome prince will always rescue the beautiful damsel in distress, and everyone lives happily ever after. After a beating or a berating session from Aunt Gerdy, I always embellish the cruelty of the bad mother and the goodness of the rescuer.

Michel's favorite fairy tale is Rumpelstiltskin. His young brother Stuart's favorite is Hansel and Gretel. Because she is sad and lonely and like me has no real mommy, my favorite is Cinderella.

How I love storytelling! I play all the parts and take on the appropriate voice for each of my roles. The boys boo the villain and clap and cheer for the hero and heroine. Stuart always falls asleep after the first hour, so Michel and I continue way past the eight o'clock curfew. It is our secret time. "Tell me another story!" he always pleads.

It pains him to watch me being ridiculed, criticized, screamed at, punished, and hit.

"You wanna play?" Michel asks after he sneaks into our bedroom. He wants to console me. "Any game you want." Other times he says, "Tell me a story." Despite his being four years younger than me, I know that he understands how humiliated and embarrassed I always feel.

Tonight, almost twenty years later, I want to stand up in this dark theater, filled with its famous and elegantly dressed premiere audience and me, sitting next to Tommy Tune, the most famous one of all. I want to shout, *I'm the sister! That should have been my life! That should have been me! Shine the spotlight over here! I'm the sister!*

I have no real identity of my own. It is a working self for dealing with the world. Behind that fake self is total chaos. I need my brother's approval. My life is small and dark. I bask in his love and fame, so I use being the *sister* of the talented, exciting, and charismatic Michel Stuart as my new identity. "Myself" is really a false self.

CHAPTER TWENTY-ONE

ONCE UPON A TIME

I enroll in a three-month Katherine Gibbs secretarial course after learning of a job opening as secretary to the assistant comptroller at the luxurious, hotel-like Doctors Hospital, where I currently work on the weekends giving out patient information in 1978. The application states that you must have experience with end-of-the month financial reports. I immediately apply, even though I have no typing skills and have never seen a month-end close report. I have trouble even balancing my checkbook.

I sit across from the Doctors Hospital chief financial officer while he talks to me about feeling trapped in a lifeless, boring, twenty-five-year marriage. This will essentially be my job interview. I am hired certainly not for my typing skills but because I have mastered the art of knowing just the right moment to offer sympathy or agreement or a comforting smile. I soon learn that my real job is to cover up for another man who will be my boss when he's at his three-hour drinking lunches and to always answer, "I'm sorry, he's in a meeting and cannot be disturbed" when his wife calls.

Thank God for Lenore, the CFO's loyal, painfully thin executive secretary who, after many months of trying and failing to teach me how to line up the numbers and type a simple one-page report, ends up typing it for me every month.

I meet Milton in 1979, six months after starting my new job. He is pacing the lobby of Doctors Hospital. I've been watching him through the glass door of my office at the far end of the lobby. He looks disoriented, so I walk over and ask him if there is anything I can do. He quietly takes hold of my arm and leads me to the wood-paneled private waiting room, where we sit on an antique, brocade-covered love seat. I wait for him to speak. Shaken and agitated, he mutters something about Pearl "getting shocked." I wait for him to calm down and he tells me that Pearl, his wife of fifty-two years, has just been admitted and will undergo a series of shock treatments. She is seventy-four, a year younger than he is, and rather fragile. He feels helpless and guilty for having consented to this aggressive treatment.

"I miss my Pearl," he whispers. "What happened to the woman who laughed at my corny jokes and who was always ready and eager to entertain, even at the last minute? Where has the mother of our three wonderful daughters gone? Where is the vibrant, beautiful wife that took care of me? What happened to my theater-loving spouse? I've lost the woman I loved."

He shakes his head in despair. "For the last ten years all she wants is to be left alone, to sit on the sofa all day. She doesn't do anything with me anymore." He has tried everything, and as a last resort her psychiatrist has recommended shock waves to her brain. He has little hope or faith that these treatments will make Pearl better. He sounds so lonely, and only when he talks about his business does he come alive.

He is a manufacturer of lingerie, with a huge showroom on Fifth Avenue and manufacturing plants in Puerto Rico,

Pennsylvania, and upstate New York. Born to and raised by Russian refugees on the Lower East Side, he founded a lingerie company, named Movie Star, fifty years ago when he was an impoverished, uneducated man of twenty-five. He brags that he has never missed a day of work, even at his age. In fact, it has become his only source of real happiness, he sadly admits. He says he is a tough boss, but with two thousand employees, he has to "run a tight ship."

I say nothing. I just listen. That's all he needs now. It would be condescending to play armchair therapist with him, pretending to know that Pearl will be fine. *Just keep quiet. Don't interrupt. Don't relate to his guilt and sadness. Don't start talking about yourself as you usually do, making the conversation all about you. Just shut up.* This is what I keep telling myself as I listen to him talk.

Sensing that I have been away from my desk far too long, I take his hand to say good-bye. He holds it tightly, as if he does not want to let go, and thanks me for listening. "Nobody has for a long time," he whispers.

Every day he comes to visit his Pearl. He seems to time his visits around my lunch hour. By the third week, I find myself waiting for him to walk through the front door and head to my office carrying our beautifully prepared lunch. We always sit on a bench in Gracie Square Park across from the hospital and next to the mayor's residence, and talk about our lives.

He is deeply moved by the commitment and devotion I show in the care of my son, but I have the feeling that he does not approve of my divorce.

"People should stay together and work it out," he tells me.

One afternoon it begins to rain. When he asks the hospital doorman to find him a cab, he reaches into his pocket for a tip and realizes that he has forgotten his wallet. "Can you lend me five dollars?" he asks me. I hurry to my office and from my pocketbook take out a small yellow envelope marked *Spending Money*. I had just that morning cashed my paycheck and, as I have been doing ever since my divorce four years earlier, I have divided it into separate little envelopes marked *Rent, Food, David's Tutors and Therapist*, and *My Therapy with Dr. Bob*. Any money left over is for a standing room ticket to the opera or a movie; I can never afford both. I rush back and hand him five dollars, expecting never to see it again. The next morning, Pearl has had an early discharge and when I arrive at work I find a box on my desk filled with long-stemmed red roses, a hundred-dollar bill stuck into one of the roses, and a scribbled note saying, "Thank you, Milton H."

That evening Jose, the elevator operator in my rent-controlled West Village apartment house, greets me with a huge grin. He waves his hand at an assortment of various-sized gift boxes scattered about on the lobby floor.

"These came for you this afternoon. They were delivered by a chauffeur."

I am quite certain that by now every tenant in the building has heard the part about the chauffeur. The lingerie in the boxes is more beautiful than any I have ever seen and nothing like the cheap, drab sweatshirt and stretch pants I usually wear to bed. The lobby floor filled with flowers, plants, and boxes of Movie Star lingerie will be a scene that gets repeated for the next five evenings. It ends only when I consent to have dinner with Milton. His chauffeur comes for us. David is wearing his cousin's hand-me-down jacket and dark-blue, slightly faded corduroy pants, and I am wearing my barely fitting size 12 black dress. The driver of the black stretch limousine is silent, but David and I are giggling in the back seat all the way to the Plaza Hotel, where the maître d' in the Oak Room escorts us to a corner table next to a picture window overlooking Central Park.

I've landed in a fairy tale. This is not real. Tomorrow I'll be Cinderella again, still fat and lonely and struggling to pay the bills.

Three months later, my son David insists that he does not want to come with me anymore. "These dinners are stupid and boring. All he does is talk to you, and when he does talk to me, I don't even understand what he's saying. Besides, I don't really care. It's the same thing every night. How happy you make him. How proud of you he is. What a good boy I am. Blah, blah, blah. Mom, I'm eleven years old. I don't need a babysitter anymore. Trust me, Mom. I can stay home alone."

Eight months later, Milton asks me to quit my job. Dinner at the Plaza four times a week is no longer enough; he now wants to have lunch with me as well. There has been no change in Pearl's deepening depression, and because she has threatened to harm herself, he's hired around-the-clock care for her now.

A rich and powerful man, used to having his own way, Milton's pursuit of me is relentless. "I am deeply in love with you," reads a card tucked into the small blue Tiffany box that holds my new gold Rolex watch.

He will not divorce Pearl, nor will he let me go. He begs me to be his companion. "I will make you happier than you have ever been. We will enroll your David in the finest private school that money can buy."

I was a lonely, traumatized orphan when I came to America. Growing up with my new family, a loving uncle and his abusive wife, I survived through the fairy tales that I told to Michel and Stuart; in that world I believed that someday a prince would come and rescue me too. Only then would I live happily ever after. I would know immediately when I found my prince because he'd have a handsome, youthful face with blond or black hair, sparkling blue or green eyes, and a muscular body. But here stood my prince—bald, short, fat, wrinkled, and seventy-five years old. As for his sparkling eyes, they hide behind glasses (even after two cataract surgeries) with lenses so thick that they'd left a permanent scar on the bridge of his long, wide nose.

I resign from my job at the hospital; a forty-year-old Cinderella has become a princess! It is not a bells ringing, head-over-heels, dizzying romantic love that I have for this wonderful man. I've never been with a man who loved and cherished me like this. This is new and unfamiliar. I am more used to being with men who only confirmed my own self-loathing back to me.

David is enrolled in a boarding school in Putney, Vermont, one dedicated to teaching learning-disabled boys how to read and write and learn the most difficult subject of all: math. Milton moves me into an enormous apartment on the Upper East Side of Manhattan and furnishes it lavishly.

By now I have become a familiar fixture in Milton's showrooms and factories in Puerto Rico, Pennsylvania, Atlanta, and, of course, New York. For weeks at a time, we stay at the Palm Aire or Harbor Island Spa in Florida. In California, we enjoy the exclusive, fantastically expensive Golden Door or the Cal-A-Vie with its private Mediterranean-style villas, or at my favorite: the less expensive Rancho La Puerto in Baja. When we visit his factory in Puerto Rico twice a year, we stay at the Dorado Beach Hotel and Golf Club.

My three-bedroom, three-bathroom New York apartment with a fireplace in the living room has three walk-in closets filled with designer clothes to wear on my massaged, pampered, dieted, tan-even-in-winter, new size 8 body. Built-in shoe racks house a hundred pairs of I. Miller, Salvatore Ferragamo, and Charles Jourdan shoes. The surrounding shelves are lined with handbags to match.

Once a month we register as man and wife at the Sherry Netherland, the Plaza, the Helmsley Palace Hotel, or the Regency Hotel on Park Avenue, where we always begin with their famous power breakfast before we head to our room, pretending that we have just married and are on our honeymoon. I, playing the role of his adored wife, have changed into my newest Movie Star lingerie and wait with open arms to embrace my virile, handsome, young, sexy man. I am so grateful for the security that my Milton gives me, something I have never had before, that to pretend that he excites me is the least I can do.

When we crave Italian food, we eat in the notoriously expensive La Caravelle or Delmonico's. When we want French food, we eat in the upscale La Côte Basque. When we eat in the huge, open room of The Four Seasons restaurant, I order a medium-rare steak and baked potato, with sour cream.

I now carry at least $500 in cash in my wallet and charge everything on my American Express Gold Card, with the bill going directly to Milton. Where I once could only afford a standing room ticket in the rear of the house, I now hold a season subscription in a reserved front row box seat at the Metropolitan Opera. I celebrate the New Year alone, listening to Strauss waltzes and sipping champagne at the New York Philharmonic. I am able to donate large sums to my favorite animal rescue, and to the Save the Children organization. I volunteer my time in hospitals, visiting sick children. To homebound seniors I bring food and a few hours of cheer. I am a regular at Carnegie Hall. Milton and I spend much of the winter in the sun. David and I summer in the Hamptons and on Fire Island. On school vacations we use Eastern Airline tickets, which Movie Star buys by the hundreds, to travel to Aruba, Jamaica, Club Med in Mexico, Disneyland, St. Thomas, the Dominican Republic's new Club Med in Punta Cana, and a private house on the beach in Bermuda. We cruise the Greek islands.

David is thirteen when we fly to Israel and Egypt. We are guests in the five-star King David Hotel and at the Mena House, another magnificent hotel in Cairo, with an awesome view of the Pyramids. During our stay I hear the rumor that President Anwar Sadat of Egypt and Israeli Prime Minister Menachem Begin had first met here to discuss the peace treaty that they signed at Camp David in 1979.

How self-conscious I felt in the first few months after we met. It embarrassed me when he'd take the starched white linen napkin from the table in the Oak Room, or The Sherry Netherland's dining room, and tie it around his neck like a bib. I cringed when he snapped his fingers at the waiters to get their attention. He smothered me with attention. His voice was gruff and loud, especially in the quiet, flower-filled dining rooms where we always ate. "She doesn't like this," he'd shout to the maître d'. "Bring her something else. I want her to be happy." No "Excuse me, please." No lowered voice so as not to draw attention. Instead, everyone stared at us, so I just turned my head and looked out the window. He left huge tips; sometimes the tip was more than the meal. The waiters fought to serve our table, and he never left the dining room before discreetly slipping a hundred-dollar bill into the palm of the maître d'.

By the end of our first year together, I have become arrogant and pompous. But behind that attitude, I am really hiding how undeserving I feel to be with this man. I envy his confidence and his ease in speaking up when he has something on his mind. He doesn't care what people think. I, of course, care too much. I am so desperate to be liked. I want people to see me as sweet and nice and good. He is never cruel or mean, just loud. His employees love him.

It is a mild fall day when Milton and I are walking back to the showroom after lunch. With the Empire State Building a block away, lower Fifth Avenue is always packed with people and backed-up traffic. It's not unusual to see young people handing out brochures advertising a new restaurant opening, a nail salon, or happy hour discounts at the sports bar down the street. One such group rushes toward us and hands us a folded yellow paper covered in large black print and a Star of David. They wear white shirts, black jackets and pants, wide black hats, and beards. Milton quickly reaches in his pocket for money, thinking these fresh-faced, smiling young men are the Chabad Lubavitch, an ultra-orthodox movement that provides housing, financial support, and counseling to runaways, troubled teens, and drug addicts. Milton is a major philanthropist, giving huge sums of money to any charity that is Jewish themed. But just as he hands the smiling young man his money, he sees the word "Jesus" in the center of the Jewish star on the brochure. "Why is Jesus here?" he asks.

The proud young man answers, "We are Jews for Jesus, sir."

Milton looks at me. "Who are these cockamamie *meshugganahs*? You should be ashamed of yourselves. Your mothers would cry if they saw you preaching this crap," he shouts. He rips the brochure up and throws it to the ground.

"I'm so proud of you," I whisper. *They are weird. How can you be a Jew and believe in a Christian Jesus?* But I am self-conscious and overly concerned that they might think badly of me. So, I just shake my head back and forth and tsk-tsk my disapproval of the young Jews for Jesus group as we walk away.

I don't know what to say or how I feel when Milton shows me the deed to the two gravesites that he bought in his family plot for David and me. I will always be with him, lying on his right and Pearl on his left. This is how he envisions his eternity. I don't know what to do with so much love. It's overwhelming. I don't know anything about being valued, respected, and adored.

The gift of the two graves that Milton bought for David and me is a simple thing. It is a small kindness for Milton, but for me this gift is huge. It brings me to tears to know that this short, thickly built, bald, old man whom I once felt ashamed to be seen with is the first man in my life that I truly love. I didn't have those bells-ringing-in-my-head, heart stopping, catch-my-breath feelings, yet my heart was ready for him and his easy, steady love for me. He is my mother, father, child, and best friend.

I am by Milton's side at the gala event when he is honored by the Board of Directors of the Jewish Guild for the Blind, for which he is a past president and donor. We lunch often with Milton's daughters, seated in the magnificent dining room of the Harmonie Club, Milton's private Jewish club on Fifth

Avenue. They thank me for spending every day with him and making their father so happy.

They thank me for the security I give them by being there to listen and to care for Milton. I watch his health, even taking him to the cardiologist that I met when I worked at Doctors Hospital. I listen to his business woes. I sympathize and try to offer comfort when he cries, "Pearl is getting worse. She does not speak. She will not leave her bed."

Milton and I agree to meet at the Oak Room of the Plaza Hotel to celebrate my return from the New Age Spa near Petaluma, California, where I spent a transformative ten days. When I enter the dining room, Sonny the maître-d' greets me with an unusually big smile. As he walks me to the table, he whispers, "I'm so glad you're back. He's been a lost puppy since you left."

Milton is beaming. "Look, my darling! I ordered your favorite!" When he lifts the silver-plated dome that is keeping my thick slice of medium-rare roast beef warm, I hear the cries of the cows in the slaughterhouse. Just days ago I was weeping and afraid to enter the slaughterhouse when our handsome, Birkenstock-shoed, vegetarian director at the New Age Spa had taken us there. I can still hear the cow's cries. I'm certain this is exactly what that spa director had in mind. I am a vegetarian now.

"Tell them to take it away right now," I demand.

Milton is embarrassed. "What's wrong?" he asks curtly.

"I will never eat an animal again," I tearfully reply. He is silent, but I know he's upset. Having my favorite meal waiting for me is how he pampers me. He is happy when he can spoil me. My outburst surprised him.

"You know I don't believe in this holistic crap," he says. "Those raisin and nut eaters are all nuts." Milton is laughing. "You get it? Nut eaters are nut cases." It's not that funny, but I'm so relieved to see him laughing that I laugh too.

"I don't care what you are or what you eat or don't eat," he says. "I love you and you love me, and that's all I care about."

CHAPTER TWENTY-TWO

MY PRINCE

Pearl dies in February 1983. A week later I wait in Milton's Fifth Avenue showroom for our usual lunch date. "Please tell Mr. Herman that I'm here," I ask the receptionist. When he comes out of his office he puts down five small boxes on the coffee table where I sit. "Pick the one you like the best," he says. Each of the five diamond rings is bigger than the other, yet it is the smallest one with the emerald cut that is my favorite.

"Let's get married right away," my Milton begs.

"We can't do that! We must show respect for Pearl. You know that Jewish law demands that we wait a year." I know he's frightened. My Milton has never lived alone, and even though Pearl was sick and depressed, at least she was there. He looks miserable. Disappointment washes over him. I feel terrible so I compromise and tell him we will get married on his birthday in November. "It's only nine months away."

* * *

It is a beautiful Sunday afternoon in August when Milton and I sit in the Palm Court of the Plaza Hotel for high tea. This beautiful atrium resembling an English garden is a welcome change from our usual Sunday afternoon brunch at the Harmonie Club. The all-you-can-eat spread is so big, the food so delicious, that like a child in a toy store, I can't choose just one or two, so I eat everything the buffet offers. Here we are served tiny little tea sandwiches. White bread without the crust cut in small squares and filled with watercress, cucumber, egg salad, or thin slices of meat. My favorite food is always the sweets. The scones, *petits fours*, and double chocolate brownies are displayed on a three-layered plate. The waiter brings it to the table on a rolling cart. I pick the brownie and a raisin scone. Milton picks the petits fours.

My Milton is bragging to complete strangers and the waiter that he and I will soon marry. He's so happy. Although he knows I won't, he pleads with me to stay in his apartment tonight. "You never stay." I know that whenever we share the same room, Milton's snores keep me from sleeping.

"No, my darling, I need to go to my own place."

That night it takes over six rings for me to answer the telephone at 1:35 a.m.

"Hello? Hello?" All I hear is heavy breathing. Frightened that it might be an obscene phone call, I quickly hang up.

This morning on August 23 is the first time in our four years together that I have not had my 8:00 a.m. "Good morning, sweetheart!" phone call from Milton. But then I remember that this is the day when he gets a massage. One hour later, when I still have not heard from him, I call the office.

"Good morning," I say to his private secretary. "Can I talk to Mr. Herman, please?"

The seconds pass like days before Gail, with choking sobs, finally blurts out, "Mr. Herman passed away early this morning!"

This cannot be! "Gail! We spent the whole day together yesterday. We had dinner ten hours ago!" I am screaming into the phone now. "He was so happy, bragging to total strangers that we are getting married, that I will finally live with him in the Hampshire House on Central Park South—'my sweetheart's favorite street'—and that he is the luckiest man in the world to be marrying such a wonderful woman. When we said good night, I promised to come to the office early to bring him his favorite breakfast of kippered herring."

I ask what time he died...though I sense that I already know. "Mr. Herman's daughter said it was at 1:40."

The "obscene phone call" had been my Milton. He had wanted to hear my voice even as he lay dying, alone in the beautiful tenth-floor, five-room apartment on my favorite street in New York, with every window overlooking Central Park.

I am shattered, in denial, and unable to move from the sofa, where I lie sobbing into Milton's blue-and-white handkerchief. He had used it to wipe the perspiration from my face two years earlier—after an eighty-two-year-old Grandma Kitty (the retired maid whom David stayed with when I was in Bellevue twelve years earlier) led me and my guests, even the young rabbi, in a hand-clapping, hip-swaying twenty-minute sing-along at David's bar mitzvah, accompanied by the orchestra she had quietly and in utmost secrecy arranged.

It is early evening when Milton's eldest daughter calls me. I am surprised to hear her voice, since she has never called before. Cool, distant, and stiff—I will call her Melissa. I have nothing more than a cordial relationship with her. Not like the one that I have with Milton's youngest daughter (whom I will call Leila), who is warm and genuine and friendly.

"Did you see my father last night?"

"Yes, we had dinner together," I answer. "Why do you ask?"

"You know that my father always carried loose checks and rolled-up hundred-dollar bills in his pants pockets. Well, the money is missing."

I'm so numb with grief that I don't realize until months later when I replay that phone conversation in my head that she had accused me of stealing the money.

I stand with Mel, Milton's friend and colleague, away from the crowd of people at the cemetery, my red and swollen eyes hidden behind dark glasses. Mel is a handsome, white-haired married man of seventy who has brought his fat and abrasive wife rather than the lovely, dark-haired, classy Israeli girlfriend whom Milton and I liked and had many dinners with.

"Schlemiel, you could have had enough money for three lifetimes," Mel begins. "You could have lived in a $10 million apartment on your favorite street. You could have given your son everything he needs in life. Kids like your David have it hard. The money you would have inherited as Milton's wife would have made life easier for you and for him. I told you, marry him right away! Are you stupid or just naïve to have insisted on waiting the year that you thought Jewish law demands, to marry an eighty-year-old man? So now you can wipe your ass with all the respect you showed his dead wife."

As the limousine drives past the Belmont racetrack on the way back from the Beth David cemetery in Elmsford, I can't help but smile. Milton loved horse racing and had tried for years to bring me with him. He had an enclosed, private, air-conditioned box. "Please come with me," he'd beg, but I would not. I'd tell him, "It's a cruel sport that I will not watch."

Well, my Milton, you finally took me to the racetrack.

CHAPTER TWENTY-THREE

FALLEN HERO

Based on the financial success and critical acclaim of *Nine*, the 1982 Tony Award-winning show Michel had produced, my thirty-nine-year-old brother asks me to invest in his new show, *The Tap Dance Kid*. Opening night will be December 21, 1983.

I had asked my Milton to please sell the Movie Star stock he had given me in celebration of my forty-third birthday on May 5, 1982. Five months later I gave Michel $52,000, the proceeds from that sale. Ten months later, my Cinderella-turned-Princess world is shattered.

I am sleepwalking. In every room of this apartment I see Milton. There is the beige velvet love seat and matching lounge he chose. There's the dishwasher that he had his decorator and workmen install in an impossibly narrow space. There are the gorgeous blue-flowered chintz armchairs and loveseat he bought in Bloomingdale's. I can't believe my Milton is dead. Somehow I never thought Milton would ever die. Secretly, I think that he is just away and that he is coming back. I am steeped in grief, and every day I go through the motions like a robot. I am lost. I feel more alone than ever. I miss my Milton. How happy I was in that life. I miss my life and I want to go back to it. I was always under my Milton's protective wing. I felt invincible. Now I feel like an orphan. Who will I be with without him?

David, now sixteen, nags me. "Mom, are you just going to sit and cry all day?" I am again the lonely girl growing up with my new family whose only comfort is food. Food was my friend. I ate to fill the empty feeling I always had. So now I cry and eat. I eat through my tears. Chocolate cake and chocolate chip cookies, strawberry shortcake, thick slices of cream cheese-filled carrot cake, Italian cheesecake, and six mini cannoli (deep-fried tubes of pastry filled with sweetened ricotta cheese).

It is all I can do to keep myself moving. Whatever energy I have I use to get dressed and apply makeup for my Sunday excursion. That's when I leave the house and take the train to Floral Park, a lovely, quiet, and middle-class neighborhood in Queens. It's the same every Sunday. First the Korean grocery store for a small bouquet of blue, pink, and yellow daisies and a small coffee. Then on to the Italian bakery one block over where I buy a small box of mini vanilla and chocolate cannoli, my comfort food. Then I must walk back to the station and into the small taxi stand to order a taxi to take me to the Beth David Cemetery. I tell the cab driver to let me off at the back gate since it is the easiest and fastest route to the grave. Then I begin my walk on the narrow streets in the cemetery that will take me to the grave.

I make a left on Lincoln, a right on Bethel, a left on Madison, a right on Judah, between Madison and Adams. In section C1 I look for Judah Avenue and find the Golde Michel Family Circle plot. My darling Milton is the newest occupant of the plot that he named for his parents. He lies to the left of his wife Pearl. His much-adored mother Golde and his browbeaten father Michel lie one row over. There is no headstone for Milton yet because Jewish law demands that it not be put up until the end of the twelve-month mourning period. I lay my bouquet on the raised mound of fresh grass at his gravesite.

I sit on the marble bench that Milton provided for this beautiful family plot, and I notice that I am wearing two different shoes and my shirt is inside out. Had no one noticed? But, this is New York, and even if they had they wouldn't care enough to tell me. I eat the cannoli and drink my coffee. I cry. I eat. I talk to my Milton. "I miss you," I cry. "I was angry when you left. But now all I feel is grateful. Thank you for loving me," I say over and over again. What a lucky woman I am! How many women have been lucky enough to have had such a fairy tale life?

I have forgotten the holistic approach to eating—that what you put in your body matters. In the four years that we'd been together, Milton and I traveled to luxurious health spas and I had taken good care of my body. Six months after Milton died, the small-waistline, flat-stomached, size 8 body I'd worked so hard to get has vanished. Nothing fits me except for one old, pre-spa, size 12 dress.

I am bombarded with telephone calls from well-intentioned friends and acquaintances offering me their unsolicited advice. "You need to get out, Sylvia. Have lunch with us. It will do you good. No more of this moping and crying!" Only nine months have passed since my Milton passed. How dare they impose their feelings and demands on me? I just let the answering machine pick up their calls. Can't they see that I am doing all that I can do to keep myself from falling apart?

I still wait to hear Milton's voice on the telephone to begin my day. "Good morning, sweetheart!" He is coming back. But no, he's not coming back. He's dead.

I call my brother Michel. I am shattered and flattened and numb. I need family.

Several weeks later, and late at night, he finally arrives. Deeply tanned, scary thin, and wearing sunglasses, Michel sweeps into the room. He's talking nonstop, almost manically, about Water Island, damn ferry, and stupid bitch. "Tommy's really over me now," Michel whines. He's making me nervous with his endless crazy chatter. When I question him about his drastic weight loss (afraid that he might have AIDS), he waves me away. He's twitchy and anxious, and keeps running his finger under his nose, as if he were wiping an invisible runny nose. I am uncomfortable. My brother is acting bizarre and scary, and I have no patience for him now.

"Stop it!" I want to scream. "Can't you see that I'm in pain?"

I'm relieved when Michel announces rather dramatically only ten minutes later, "My friends are waiting in a limo and I *need* to go now," and wearing a thin phony smile and the sunglasses he hadn't taken off the entire time, he walks out the door.

* * *

Ten months after my Milton died, a thickly packed envelope from a law office arrives. The documents say that before his death, Milton had added a handwritten, notarized note to his will. It states that the Milton Estate will be responsible for the sum of $92,000 for David's education. This will include room, board, and tuition to the Darrow School in New Lebanon, New

York, and four years at a private college for young people with special learning needs.

But what I read on page six is that Milton's daughters (the Estate) will not honor his wish. The estate lawyer tells me to sign and agree to the family's generous offer of *$7,500* yearly for a state college and only after I apply for financial aid. I am stunned, angry, tired, and too wrapped up in grief to fight, so I sign. I am also notified that Milton's family took away my health insurance, my dental insurance, my life insurance, the two treasured burial plots, and of course the American Express Gold Card. But they cannot take away the happy, life-giving love we had. And, there will be no money for the Darrow School, which David needs to finish before he can even apply to the state college.

Milton and I never talked about death. It felt cold and impersonal and too calculating to even consider discussing the possibility. "What if you die, Milton?" It felt wrong to ask him that. What will happen to me and to David? I was living a life that I had only seen in the movies or in the romance magazines of my youth. I couldn't stop myself from believing that it was always going to be that way. When I read what my Milton had intended to leave for David and me, I want to call and say "thank you."

But I cannot do that, so I call my brother. "Michel, I have no money. I know you must have enough investors now, so can I get my $52,000 investment back? David has to stay at Darrow. It's his senior year."

I do not know he is an addict high on cocaine when he answers, "I cannot do that."

CHAPTER TWENTY-FOUR

PROOF OF ANGELS

By late December 1984, I've sold or auctioned off most of the gifts that Milton gave me, including the diamond ring and the double strand of perfect one-millimeter hanging pearls with a beautiful clasp made from a diamond-and-emerald brooch that had once belonged to his late wife Pearl. To a private gallery in Philadelphia I sell my signed "Slalom" LeRoy Neiman serigraph and the four signed and numbered prints of the original Art Deco Erte. Only two of the three Boulanger lithographs are sold at the William Doyle auction house. I bring my redlined mink coat and the blond mink jacket to Ritz Furs on 57th Street. "Gently used furs," say the ads. "You don't need a million to look like a million." The owner offers me five hundred dollars. I am desperate for money, but I know he'll get at least $2,500 for my furs, so I take them back home.

I'm still $8,000 short of the $20,00 in tuition money that David needs for his senior year at Darrow. I could not, even though it would have brought me an additional three or four thousand dollars, sell Milton's first gift to me, the magnificent emerald ring set in white gold and encircled in diamonds that I wear on the middle finger of my left hand.

I first encounter Ernie, the CEO of the United Jewish Appeal Federation (UJA), in a 1985 *People* magazine article I read in the waiting room of my doctor's office. He's pictured sitting on a railroad track with the familiar *Arbeit Macht Frei* (Work Makes Free) sign in the background above the entrance of Auschwitz. This is the death camp that Ernie had survived more than forty years earlier at age eighteen. How hard it had been for him to journey back to the place of such pain, horror, and loss, but this visit had somehow lightened him. He has devoted his life to helping the survivors and to preserving the memory of the Holocaust. His message pierces my heart: Never forget.

I like Ernie the minute I hear his voice on the phone. I'd written him a letter a month after I'd read the article. I couldn't get that article out of my mind. I'd never expected him to reply.

He welcomes me with a smile as I enter his office in the UJA building on East 59th Street. The walls are covered with pictures, including Ernie and a smiling President Reagan; Ernie and Golda Meir, Yitzhak Rabin, and Menachem Begin, the former prime ministers of Israel. His office is crammed full of awards and plaques from dignitaries and celebrities. Letters of gratitude from Holocaust survivors are spread out everywhere I look. I'm in a kind of trance of disbelief that I'm here, when Ernie says, "I hope you like Italian food."

I'm self-conscious and intimidated to be sitting in a dimly lit, somewhat garishly decorated Italian restaurant with the CEO of the largest Jewish organization in the world. Me in my cheap, wide-skirted, size 14 polyester dress, and Ernie in a shirt and tie and a light gray suit that looks like silk. I am tongue-tied when I try to speak, but Ernie puts me at ease. His heavy German-accented voice is soft, even comforting somehow. He feels like family. On every visit, Ernie gives me a warm embrace, full of hope and promise.

But, eight months later I need more than a warm embrace and lunch at Gino's restaurant. "Ernie, I don't have anything of any value left to sell. My son will not graduate. I don't know what else to do."

"I will help you. But, Sylvie"—I love when he says my name like that—"it will be our secret. I could lose my job if my colleagues or the Federation Board discovered that I have helped you." He tells me of his plan to provide me with a list of names of the UJA's most generous donors. "I want you to write a letter to each one telling them why you need their help."

As soon as I come home, I sit down to type.

Dear Sir/Madam:

My name is Sylvia Kleinman and I am 47 years old and a single mother. What a privilege it has been to share my life with my 17-year-old son David. He was 7 when he was diagnosed with a learning disability. I worked three jobs a week for five years in order to pay for the tutors, the therapist, and for the special foods he needed on the Feingold diet, which he followed after I refused to put him on Ritalin, a drug commonly prescribed for hyperactive kids.

I have survived the Holocaust, the murder of my family, and the death of the man I loved. His hand-written codicil that he had his lawyer notarize and add to the will, a week before he died, stated that he would make David's education possible. He was leaving enough money for David to finish his senior year of high school and four years of college. The estate lawyer has notified me that the family will not honor his wishes. I do not have the tuition money to pay for David's senior year. My heart is breaking. He has done so well and worked so hard. That is the reason for this letter.

I know life is hard for us now but David and I will get through it. We always have. Thank you for listening to my plea. We do really appreciate anything you can do to help.

One week later, Ernie says, "This letter is very good. Here are the names that I promised you. Send them this letter along with a picture of your son."

It does not take long, maybe two or three months, before the checks begin to arrive. Each one is attached with a note that reads, "I hope in some small way that this has contributed to the well-being of your son David." All ten Jewish foundations and private individuals have generously responded to my plea.

* * *

When I watch David walk onto a darkened stage at the high school graduation ceremony a year later, I reflect on the unbelievable circumstances that have delivered us to this moment—a mother fighting for her son, a man who gave me a secret list and risked losing his job, and the strangers who donated $8,000 to enrich the life of this eighteen-year-old boy.

Today, he is standing in the spotlight, holding the guitar he taught himself to play, announcing, "I wrote this melody for my mom. I call it 'Miracle.'"

CHAPTER TWENTY-FIVE

HOMELESS

It is 1986 and I am $50,000 in debt from the failed day spa I opened last year, on the eleventh floor of an office building on Wall Street. It was one floor above the infamous Ivan Boesky of insider trading fame and a donor on that UJA list who had mailed a check for $250 with a note that read, "I was very moved by your letter but this is my only and final contribution."

Following David's graduation I had enrolled at the Christine Valmy School of Cosmetology on Fifth Avenue, six blocks away from the big-windowed Movie Star showroom where I once waited daily for my Milton to take me to lunch. I learned how to do facial treatments, how to apply makeup, and how to operate a business. Six months later I am a New York State-licensed esthetician and I rent a facial chair in a small, windowless room of John's Hair Salon on Wall Street.

All my hopes and dreams and enthusiasm went into opening Silvie's Day Spa, the first day spa on Wall Street. I did not have a business plan; actually I didn't have *any* plan. A good friend who worked at a bank helped me get a loan. It was a personal loan with a high interest rate; that's all I could get. I had no credit cards and no collateral. The two dark rose-colored manicure tables with matching chairs, the fancy steamer, and the faux leather, rose-colored facial chair I leased, at an even higher rate.

I would cater to the busy, stressed-out men and women in the financial district. They would be pampered in lavender-and-rose decorated rooms, with classical music softly floating through hanging speakers. I would offer healing aromatherapy facials; relaxing body massages, makeup lessons and application, and my private-label skin care products for sale. There would be hot oil manicures and pedicures, from Anna and Irene. I had only $1,000 in seed money. I took the Movado watch off my wrist and grabbed the self-winding steel Datejust Oyster Rolex out of my bag and used them to barter with the architect. I was not taking a salary and I was spending more than Silvie's was bringing in. Not even my twelve-hour days, or standing outside handing out flyers that said "Free Facials!" or the soothing sensation of my magic hands, or my prayers were enough to keep Silvie's Day Spa open.

I have managed (barely) to pay the rent on the rent-controlled apartment Milton moved me to. The notice says that the building will soon be undergoing a co-op conversion—with a separate clause that states that should a tenant choose not to buy, they can stay on as a renter, but they will give up the option of ever buying it and becoming a shareholder. My apartment is priced for insiders, residents already living in the building, at $250,000—money I do not have.

I find a real estate agent. She works for a respected East Side firm. "A large three-bedroom, three-bathroom, with a working fireplace, on the Upper East Side will not take long to sell," she says. I sign a six-month contract. Three months later she brings me the buyer, a lovely, dark-haired executive from Bloomingdale's. I sell at my insider price of $250,000 (that check is made out to Bing and Bing, the family who owns this beautiful building), to which my buyer writes another check for $250,000 that is for me. I am heartbroken that I have to leave my beautiful home.

After I pay the broker, the real estate agent, the lawyer, my Silvie's spa furniture lease, and my bank loan, I pack my bag. The movers pick up my books and a couple of pieces of furniture that remained after my moving sale. I grab the $200,000 cashier's check and my airline ticket to San Diego—the city I picked because it is only two hours away from the Guitar Institute in Los Angeles, where David lives and studies—and leave for the airport.

CHAPTER TWENTY-SIX

LOVE AND MEMORY

I have left my beloved New York behind, and I am still sobbing even as the taxi pulls up to the small, two-month rental house that the Century 21 agent in La Jolla has found for me.

It's an ugly, dark house, furnished with ugly, dark, old stuff. What have I done? I need to go home. But I have no home. I am stranded, trapped, and totally alone.

I begin unpacking the boxes that I had sent from New York. Three cartons hold my favorite books. The fourth box I have packed with photographs. I lay them out on the table. Taken in 1943, one black-and-white photograph shows my two sisters and me after we were smuggled into Switzerland. Rita has her arm around me. Hot tears run down my cheeks as I gaze at the photo.

Secretly I now wish that my cousin Herbert could do one more rescue mission, like the one he did that morning in 1963 after my final breakup with Freddy, and deliver me into Rita's waiting arms.

"Rita, I hate it here," I whine to my sister in our weekly phone call. "Everyone smiles *all the time*. The women look like the Stepford Wives, and just like the ones in the movie, they only smile with their lips. It's scary. People can't be this happy all the time."

La Jolla's sidewalks and streets are so clean I could eat off them. It has no subway, no bus, and I have to phone when I need a cab. I'm forty-eight years old and now I have to learn how to drive. I think I have landed on some strange, new planet. I miss the traffic, the honking of the horns, and the cabbies shouting a "Fuck you!" or "Hey, asshole, can't you see the light's red?"

"Rita, I don't belong here."

But Rita is silent. She does not respond to my litany of complaints. My conversation seems to baffle her. Instead she tells me about old friends who died years ago as though she had seen them yesterday. Her words run together. When I try changing the topic it is hard for her to follow. In a panicked rush to get her thoughts out, she speaks to me in German, the language of her childhood, and one she has not uttered to me in over fifty years. I pretend not to hear the fear in her voice as she spins her obsessive tales of the past. I try to reel her back to me. "Rita, I need your help!" But she keeps babbling. "Rita, please pull yourself together," I plead.

After spending the last ten years in Miami as part-time snowbirds, Rita has finally convinced her husband to retire and give up the bitter cold winters of Ohio. Two years ago, they bought a condo in North Miami Beach, which Rita furnished with expensive white wicker, not the heavy dark wood of the house in Cleveland. Yet she could not resist covering every empty space with white plastic doilies and vases stuffed with plastic flowers, her *tchotchkes*.

It's the wraparound balcony that overlooks the Olympic-size pool that she treasures the most. At age fifty-three, still young enough to enjoy it, Rita will finally have the good life all year round, lying in the sun until her skin is baked dark brown, sitting poolside and playing cards with the "girls," ages fifty to eighty.

I hope she cannot detect my lack of interest and impatience as I listen to her many complaints and fears, but selfishly only my petty problems concern me now.

"I have terrible back pain, I see funny spots in front of my eyes, and sometimes I feel dizzy and I hear this strange ringing in my ear," she says. "The doctor did some kind of scan of my brain and my spine. He didn't see anything wrong. He said I was just depressed. I take the pills but I'm still sad."

Three months later she tells me, "The last time I went in the pool my leg cramped up. I was so scared. I thought I would drown." By now her voice is louder, and she is crying. "I don't go outside; the sun is too hot and it hurts my eyes. I don't go anymore. I stopped playing cards, I can't concentrate, and those women get on my nerves. I just like to stay in the apartment, with the blinds closed, and watch my soap operas."

I see that my selfish whining of helplessness is an intrusion on *her* needs now. My needs are much smaller here, and my heart aches for her.

"Rita-leh, it's common for women to get depressed when their grown children leave the house. Maybe you're going through menopause," I suggest, forgetting that she'd had a hysterectomy many years ago.

"Sometimes, I don't remember where I put the key that starts the car. Other times I am at the grocery store and ready to pay, but I forgot to take money with me. I forget to put soap in the washing machine. What's wrong with me?" she cries.

"Honey, there's nothing wrong with you. I forget things all the time. Maybe you just had other things on your mind. In fact last Tuesday I forgot my wallet. Luckily the bagel shop knows me so I paid for my lunch the following day. Please, stop being so hard on yourself," I add.

This is not mild depression, I fear. My strategy will be to try and neutralize it all. The tone I choose to use is perfectly normal. I have to find the cause, the hidden reason for this unwelcome intruder, this darkness that has overcome her, that has stolen my happy sister.

"I can't walk right," she tells me two months later.

"What does that mean?" I ask.

"The right leg, it drags. It tingles. Sometimes it feels like there are pins and needles sticking me."

I have to think fast. There are answers that comfort and answers that make it worse. My sister's sense of safety rests on my ability to absorb my fear and concern, and sound as if everything is fine. "Rita-leh, your leg just fell asleep. You probably sat too long with your legs crossed."

When she tells me that her son Mark had come to visit and she could not remember his name when introducing him to her neighbor, I can offer no explanation, no excuse, no way to have it make sense, no words of solace. I have run out of things to say.

CHAPTER TWENTY-SEVEN

MR. WRONG

Six months later, a tall, gorgeous young man is flirting with me in the garden of the bagel shop in La Jolla. My gentle three-year-old rescued dachshund is sitting on my lap and thinks that this hunk is standing much too close and that he might hurt me. (Elmo may be a dog but he *is* a male—jealous and possessive.) Out comes Elmo's inner pit bull in full protection mode for his beloved human. We laugh as my sweet dog bares his teeth and growls. I'm smiling when I remember how the lady at the shelter had warned, "He's dangerous! Be careful or he'll lick you to death."

On our first date later that week, Elmo and I ride in Peter's red Isuzu pickup truck to the Bluffs, his favorite spot. The rocky cliffs look down on a great expanse of blue a thousand feet below. I am in awe of this breathtaking site.

"Thank you for sharing it with me," I whisper when he grabs me in his arms. With Elmo barking furiously at my feet, Peter kisses me.

His mouth is warm and smells like peppermint. I lean into him, nearly collapsing. My legs feel like rubber bands and I've dropped Elmo's leash. Peter has to hold me up. Butterflies are flapping in my stomach and I can't breathe. You'd think I was fifteen and not forty-nine.

He is twenty-four. Three years older than my son. His eyes are a bluish gray, like the color of a razor blade. They have the same polished shine.

I'm lonely and vulnerable. I miss New York. I'm worried about my sister. My only friends here are Noreen, the short, pear-shaped, single mom who waitresses in the bagel shop; Mr. Chennault, my warm and patient Jamaican driving instructor; my Century-21 agent who had rented me that ugly, dark house when I first arrived, but who has now sold me my beautiful, new townhouse; and my sweet dog Elmo.

This fabulous-looking young man who is attracted to me is just the distraction I need now. I imagine myself with him by my side. Peter's attention will quiet down the white noise in my head. *You're old and fat. I will show those young, toned, tanned, blonde-haired California girls that I'm sexy and attractive. You can prove it, Sylvia. A beautiful young man three years older than your son is wild about you.* I am ripe for some excitement. I'm ready prey.

Two months later, holding a large black gym bag and a six-pack of Corona beer, Peter moves into my two-story townhome.

We are standing in front of the movie theater. A visibly uncomfortable and embarrassed Peter is holding me in his arms while I sob nonstop about the romantic story and deliciously happy ending of *Moonstruck*, the movie we've just seen. Maybe it is my tears that touch his young heart or maybe he just wants me to stop my crying when he blurts out, "Please, let me take care of you. Marry me."

"Yes," I say. Yes, oh, absolutely yes, I want to be married to you, my gorgeous young construction worker. You are sweet, you are totally hilarious when you read me *Calvin and Hobbes*, the comic strip you love, and you are beautiful. There is no doubt about it. Yes. No more loneliness and no more self-loathing chatter in my head. We will be a couple. I need that security of hearing "my husband," "my wife," because these two phrases make me feel like I have come into a safe harbor.

A swelling tide of desire and lust sweeps any sense of reason away. What am I doing? I don't know; only my body knows. The danger of marrying a man half my age is such a turn-on that I even tell myself it's love.

Under an orange sunset sky, in the gazebo in Embarcadero Park, and with the interfaith rabbi from the Jewish Fellowship Center of San Diego presiding, we marry two months later. Peter is twenty-five and I am fifty. Elmo is "best dog" for my groom, the delicious young creature at whom my dog still growls.

Peter arrives on his skateboard, wearing the new Hawaiian shirt I'd bought him and holding a small bouquet of handpicked flowers for his happy bride. And here I am married, but six months later I am feeling more alone than when I was alone. The shyness and naïveté that I had found so refreshing and dear is boring me to death. It was so sweet when he'd visit me on his skateboard at the La Jolla salon where I work. Now I'm embarrassed and ashamed of his childish behavior. If I have to listen to another *Calvin and Hobbes* joke I will explode. His lovemaking is like an amateur, and is no longer as delightful as it had been. *To make love to a woman, shouldn't you pay attention to her?* I wonder. In the passion of that moment when Peter said, "Marry me," the first thing to go had been my perspective. I should have listened to Elmo. He'd always known that Peter was Mr. Wrong.

I file for divorce.

CHAPTER TWENTY-EIGHT

AWAKENING

The address is scribbled on an order slip, tucked into the bottom of the bag I used on that bright April morning. It says: "Torrey Pines Christian Church Co-Dependents Anonymous." Noreen from the bagel shop had given it to me three months earlier. "Check this place out," she said, pressing the paper into my palm.

Just before twelve-thirty, I open a heavy door where there is a small sign with an arrow pointing to a narrow flight of stairs down to the basement. The crucifix above the door of the brightly lit room makes me nervous. The only time I've been in a Christian church was on Christmas Eve for midnight mass with my friends in New York. My heart is pounding as I scan the crowded room for a seat.

A woman about my age is sitting across from me.

"Hi, I'm Louise, and I am a grateful recovering co-dependent."

"Hi, Louise," the whole room responds in a loud, clear boom.

I hunch down in my folding chair and I want to bolt. But I'm afraid that someone will drag me back in and the whole room will point at me and laugh. I sink deeper until I can barely read the hanging white burlap sign. *Welcome to Co-Dependents Anonymous, a fellowship of men and women whose common purpose is to develop healthy, loving relationships.* There's a beautiful young woman sitting across the aisle from me. I think I recognize her from the news station I watch. She's leaning forward, listening intently to Louise. Everyone is focused on Louise except me. I count thirty-five heads in this room. All the folding chairs are filled, and there are some people sitting on the floor.

Louise starts to tell her story.

"I could not bear silence. I had to create chaos and excitement to fill the void or else I would disappear. I slept with men because I just wanted to be held."

My palms are clammy, my stomach is constricting, and I want my heart to stop hammering. I can't sit still.

"I had no boundaries," says Louise. "I could mold myself into whatever shapes my partners, or my boss, or my friends wanted me to be. I believed that their needs were so much more important than mine. If the relationship failed I was to blame, and then I'd beat myself up because I had not tried hard enough. My men had to be flashy, exciting, handsome, and a little off. Boring was much too normal for me."

Did Noreen call her? I wonder. Did Louise know I was coming? Is she an actress pretending to be talking about her life, when it's really my life she's sharing? How does she know that this is how I feel?

People raise their hands and Louise calls on them. A cordless mic is passed around the room. They talk in clichés, some more annoying than others: "Let go and let God" and "Higher Power." I hear words like "powerless" and "denial."

After each person shares, everyone applauds as if we're at the La Jolla Playhouse. My first impulse is to leave this meeting. This is too much psychobabble and spiritual mumbo jumbo for me.

I look around the room with something bordering on self-righteous or loathing, and think: What am I doing in this room with these people who talk all this Christian stuff? I'm a Jew. I feel alien in this crowd—a horrible feeling, and a strangely familiar one too. I am trapped. I look at my watch. Thirty-five minutes and this meeting will be over.

The girl that I recognized from TV takes the microphone and announces that CODA has no dues or fees, but it does have expenses, so she's passing a basket around the room. I put a dollar bill on top of the pile. "This is a closed meeting of Co-Dependents Anonymous," she says, reading from a two-sided paper brochure. "What is said here stays here. The only requirement for membership is a desire for healthy and loving relationships."

"Is anyone here for the first time who would like to introduce themselves?" she asks.

I feel that everyone is looking at me. I stare at the floor.

As the meeting winds down, everyone applauds and then they stand. People on either side of me grab my hands as Louise says she'd like to close the meeting with the Serenity Prayer. "God," the whole room chants, "grant me the serenity to accept the things I cannot change, the courage to change the things I can, and the wisdom to know the difference."

Then they chant, "Keep coming back. It works, if you work it." They sound like cheerleaders at halftime.

Clutching the brochure I grabbed off the table, I'm almost out the door when I feel a hand on my arm. "This is your first meeting," the stranger clutching my arm says. I nod. "I had that same, frightened, what-am-I-doing here look when I first came," she adds. I don't want to talk to this woman. I just want to leave, so I lie and say, "I'm sorry but I have to run or I'll be late for my appointment."

"Keep coming back!" she shouts as I run out the door.

And so I do. I leave Elmo in the car with the windows open, and we do two meetings a day. "Let's go to a meeting, Elmo," and he jumps up to the passenger seat and off we go. I call the small white Toyota hatchback my Elmo car.

I'm horrified when I learn that I'm not loving and generous. I am plagued by jealousy and scorekeeping, and filled with self-loathing. I am a caretaker and people-pleaser. I am shut down and have no boundaries. I am obsessed and I worry constantly about other people's feelings. I have no true self. I let others define me and look to men or places to rescue me. I am like a chameleon. I change myself to win approval. I am the fat girl in love with the romance of self-destruction. Or I am the girl who believes that men will save her. And I am the woman whom others see as kind, selfless, and all giving. But there is fury seething beneath the surface of my lovely smile. That even after I give and give, I get nothing for myself. Sometimes the pain in the room is nearly unbearable. I was wounded and filled with shame and self-hate when I first walked into that room. And fifteen months later, here in a Twelve Step meeting I hear the voice of God.

"Go to Rita," it says.

"Sell my house, I am moving to Miami," I tell the sweet Century 21 real estate agent who had sold it to me.

CHAPTER TWENTY-NINE

BECAUSE I
REMEMBER LOVE

David is twenty-one and has dropped out of the Guitar Institute of Technology in Los Angeles. He had dreamed of being a rock star, but after six months of long days in class and long nights spent practicing, that dream has faded. There will be no more money coming from Milton's estate (the final $7,500 tuition payment went to the Guitar Institute), so my son has no choice but to live with me again. Together we move to Florida.

The sky is as clear as glass. The sun is shining on the December morning in 1989, when David, Elmo, and I arrive. I have come to rescue my once-happy Rita from her anxiety and fear. I will recapture all the years when we sat in her big Cleveland kitchen and I begged to hear the stories about my parents and the early years of a life I don't remember.

Rita's smiling face is still framed by that dyed red hair, sprayed and teased and in her usual flip. Her clip-on earrings still match the color of her dress. I see her earrings and freshly coiffed red hair as tiny hopeful signs that maybe her depression is just temporary. She takes small, careful, wide steps when she walks into my open arms. My smile is frozen; it hides my fear when I see her deteriorated gait.

Friday is when her husband Jack sets the dinner table, as Rita and I recite the prayer and light the Sabbath candles in Mama's silver candelabra, the one that was returned to Rita in 1976 by a distant cousin in Berlin. She had promised to keep it safe after my family fled to France two weeks after the Nazis burned down the synagogues and destroyed the glass storefronts of the Jewish-owned shops in 1938—*Kristallnacht*, the Night of Broken Glass.

I buy the freshly baked challah at the Kosher Mart. The chicken soup Rita made earlier in the day and put in the fridge so that the fat could rise to the top to be spooned off is slowly simmering on the stove. I do not tell her that I am now a vegetarian, since I know that she always made this soup for me. I was the only one who liked to suck on the bones and chew off the fat from the chicken's feet. The soup bowls are stacked up next to the stove, so Rita can ladle the soup into the bowl. It is my job to carry each bowl to its rightful place. The soup is followed by thick slices of brown, gravy-soaked brisket of beef with noodles and potatoes. Every week we have our Friday night candle lighting and dinner at Rita and Jack's top floor apartment of the Berkeley Towers in North Miami Beach.

Six months later, I meet Carmen. She is Rita's new housekeeper. Three times a week she will cook. Jack, myself, and Susi, who has lived in Miami since 1983, will fill in on the days she is not here. Carmen is a pretty, chubby, affectionate Cuban woman in her early fifties who does not know what it means when I say I am a vegetarian. "I don't eat meat," I explain.

Susi now brings the freshly baked challah bread from the bakery where she works. Rita and Susi are separated by only a year. They are best friends, but I hardly know this pretty, greenish-gray-eyed, blond-haired, fifty-three-year-old woman. I have never lived under the same roof with my sister Susi, except in the three years after I was born. Susi has a round face, full, cupid-shaped lips, and Mama's green, almond-shaped eyes. They could have been twins. Rita is the female version of Papa, with his narrow face, his thin lips, and a short, thin nose. I don't look like anyone. Susi always joked that I must have come from the "mailman," an old rumor that my Uncle Julius had spread. I heard the sarcasm in her voice. It always made me feel as if she, Rita, Mama, and Papa were the *real* family. I was the pathetic outsider desperately trying to be included. Age has mellowed Susi. And now when we talk I hear the respect and love in her voice for me.

It is Mother's Day. Jack, Susi, David, and I are taking Rita to her favorite Italian restaurant—the vast, gilded, gold-and-black wallpapered, crystal-chandeliered La Paloma.

Susi and I take turns feeding her. Her hands shake and she can no longer hold her fork. Her words have become slurred and difficult to understand.

One year later she is mute and using a cane, then a walker, and then a wheelchair. Finally she is bedridden. Fifty-seven years young, Rita is diagnosed with a degenerative brain condition that has robbed her of her mind. A slow, inexorable slide into what we are told is early dementia-related Alzheimer's disease.

When she is rushed to the hospital with an upper respiratory infection, I am not included in the meeting when Susi and Rita's family agree to place her in a nursing home.

I feel helpless that I cannot offer Rita a home, but I hope that by visiting every day, I can bring home to her. I don't recognize her mind now. I don't know where it goes or how it works—so

I tell her the beautiful stories she always shared with me. They stretch back decades to Berlin, when she was young with Mama and Papa and our sister Susi.

"Remember how New York's Central Park always reminded you of the Sunday walks in Berlin's beautiful Tiergarten Park? Remember the family picnics with Uncle Levy, who you and Susi called Uncle Paldo, and Grandmother and Grandfather Gutmann in the Grünewald?"

I tell her about the wondrous *Weihnachten,* the Christmas-decorated windows of the famous KaDeWe (the Kaufhaus des Westens), the largest and oldest department store in all of Europe and the one that Mama loved most of all but could not afford.

Then I tell her my two favorite stories. "Remember the story about the red thread and garlic that Mama hung around my neck the day I was born in the Catholic hospital in Belgium to keep the evil spirits away? How helpless Papa had felt that he could not be there because he looked too Jewish? And the one about how Papa loved to kiss my thighs in between the rolls of baby fat and how I'd squeal with delight?" I had always begged for this story. "Tell me again, Rita, how much my parents loved me. Tell me again how happy I was back then!"

These are the stories of a life that have been airbrushed into my memory. I had heard them so many times in Cleveland, sitting with Rita in the big eat-in kitchen of her home.

Rita and I have unusual conversations. I know nothing but words; Rita knows everything but has no words.

She does not remember me. I remember her, and that is what really matters.

CHAPTER THIRTY

YOU BEFORE ME

The first nursing home is called the Florida Club. The name gives one the illusion that it is gorgeous and fancy, almost like a country club. But in reality, the building is filthy with every floor reeking of urine. Rita's room is barren and dark. In the drab orange and brown dining room, with its cracked and dirty cream-colored linoleum floor, thirty emaciated patients are strapped to wheelchairs. Ignored, they are drooling or shouting for help as a television entertains the aides.

After dinner I wheel Rita outside to the old majestic tree. It is surrounded by two dying potted plants in a small circle of faded grass with a small bench. There, I comb her faded red hair, apply her favorite pink lipstick, having lined and enlarged her small lips as she always did, and of course I snap on the earrings that match her housedress.

One evening I am late in bringing Rita back to her room and the aide is angry with me. She complains about a television show she wants to watch but now cannot, for she has to get my sister ready for bed. I apologize and quickly offer to get Rita ready myself. I roll Rita over on her side so that I can wash her. That's when I see the bedsore. I hold down my scream, so as not to frighten her, but I feel myself getting nauseous and dizzy at the sight. Deep and large, it is oozing blood and pus. It has probably come from sitting in a wet diaper all day. The staff tells me they only have a limited supply of cloth diapers available and that it is not possible to change the patients more than twice a day.

"Listen, bitch," Rita's husband screams at me through the phone. "It costs too much money to buy Pampers. If you want her to wear them so badly, you buy them. Besides, she doesn't feel the pain. Now get off my back about this."

I am stunned by his words. I don't recognize the once-generous, once-devoted, sixty-two-year-old man that I have known for forty-one years. Now he is the starving thirteen-year-old boy in the Lodz ghetto who was shipped to Auschwitz and forced to watch his mother and beloved four-year-old brother marched to the crematorium there. At age seventeen, a week before his liberation from the camp, Jack stood helpless and guilt-stricken as his father, whom he had kept alive with stolen bread, was beaten to death by a Nazi guard. Jack is damaged and wounded; yet I am not able to bring forth the compassion, sympathy, and understanding that I have always shown him. I am fighting for my sister.

"Don't you dare treat her like a thing!" I scream back. "She's not dead yet."

Susi and I buy the Pampers. I am happy to take on the rank mess of the caring. I polish her nails, clean her bedsore, and wipe away her feces. I wash her, apply lotion, powder her, and diaper her. I make her smile, comb her once flaming-red hair—now brittle, dry, and gray—and wheel her outside where the sun can shine on her still wrinkle-free face. I talk nonstop for hours so that her eyes open wide like saucers and look like sparkling stars.

"Rita, don't be afraid. Let go of this horrible life," I tell her. "Mama and Papa and your happy childhood in Berlin are waiting for you." Yet even when I make that promise and want so much for God to show my sister mercy and release her from this horrible life, I am still afraid to let her go.

Susi's son Michael comes through for us. He is an executive in an assisted-living corporation, and with the help of his many connections, he has Rita placed in another nursing home. It is a newly constructed one-story stucco building with a red brick roof that resembles a Spanish *hacienda*. She is put into Room 405. There is a new aide who seems kind and gentle. At last, I feel my sister will be well taken care of.

Visiting hours are over when I walk into Rita's room one night and see the aide with her arm raised, shouting for Rita to shut up. My sister is lying naked in a soiled bed with eyes that look wild with fear. I lunge toward the aide, screaming, "How dare you dishonor and degrade her this way! She is a person, not a room number. She is a Holocaust survivor and my hero!"

Later that night, I get a call from Jack. "I heard you made a scene today. If you don't quiet down and behave, I will prevent you from seeing her," he threatens.

When I arrive the next morning I am told that Rita's husband has given orders that should I make another demand or voice a concern regarding my sister, I will not be allowed to take her outside, and I will be denied any information or say in her care.

I'm shocked, embarrassed, and ashamed. I've been reprimanded. "You're a bad girl," a familiar theme. Okay, Jack, I'll shut up. But I'll never shut down. "I will never stop fighting for my sister," I mutter under my breath.

I hide Elmo in his doggie carrier and take the two buses to visit my sister. The patients love to see his fat, low-to-the-ground body walk over to them. Drooling mouths, shaking arms held out for hugging, and twisted fingers ready for stroking. Smelly laps ready for holding. With sweaty cheeks smeared with caked-on breakfast, they wait for a doggie kiss or two. Mrs. Weingarten shouts, "Bring him here, here on my lap. You know he looks just like my Schatzi," she tells me for the hundredth time as I wipe her drool off Elmo's head.

I secretly feel that no one but me has Rita's best interests at heart. I beg her family not to let them insert the feeding tube. "Please, don't do this. She has suffered long enough. Don't violate her anymore. Now is the time to let her go."

"I will not do that," her husband answers. I tell him that I know from his children that he is having an affair with the Polish woman he'd hired while Rita was still living at home. "I don't judge you, Jack. I know how lonely you are." He is lost and devastated. He has lost his best friend, the beautiful, vibrant woman he has loved since the day they first met. "Please, Jack, let her go," I beg.

"Letting Rita go would look like I killed her because of this woman," he hisses.

I need louder, stronger, more authentic voices to help me in my fight to let Rita go. I will ask her children to help.

"Will you help me?" I ask her oldest son at dinner one night. "You are the most sensitive one. You are more like your mother. You know she would not want to live like this."

"I know. My mom used to talk about that a lot. I wouldn't want to live like that."

"Please talk to your father," I beg.

"No, I'm going to stay out of this."

"You know how impressed your father is by titles. You're a New York lawyer," I beg Rita's middle son on the phone. "Your father respects you. Please ask him to let your mother go."

"I don't want to get involved," he answers.

I call her daughter in Colorado. "You're my last hope," I tell her. "You are your father's favorite. He will do anything for you. Please tell him to let your mother go!"

"Auntie, I am three months pregnant. I want my mother to meet my baby."

The tube is inserted the following morning.

I am devastated and forced to learn again the hard lesson of acceptance. I stop asking why. It does no good.

CHAPTER THIRTY-ONE

THE BUTTERFLY EFFECT

I am helpless. All I can do for Rita is to be here with her. I begin to have a recurring dream in which Rita's aide has accidentally forgotten to turn the feeding tube machine back on after giving Rita her nightly sponge bath.

And one evening as I enter her room, I see that it has happened. Just like in my dream, the machine is really in the "off" position. Rita's eyes are closed, and thinking she is asleep, I sit on her bed.

"Your life is in my hands. I can set you free and release you. No one can accuse me of wrongdoing. I will just say that I hadn't noticed that the machine was off." Afraid that I might wake her, I leave the room to pray.

"Please, God, I need your help. Give me a sign. Tell me what to do."

Rita smiles at me when I re-enter the room. She is happy to see me. I know she does not remember who I am, yet she knows I am someone who loves her.

I see the trust in Rita's eyes as a sign from God. I think about what would happen if someone would discover what I did. I imagine myself being incriminated in my sister's death. Fearing incarceration and the loss of *my* liberties, I am rendered powerless and unable to release *her*. I do not keep silent.

"Lulu! Lulu!" I scream for the aide. "This machine is off."

Rita still sips life through a feeding tube now.

I live with my son David in an apartment in Miami Beach and rent a room in Kenneth's Beauty Salon, where I give facial treatments and body massages. Seven years after Milton's death, I take the beautiful red-lined, blond mink bomber jacket— made for me by Max the furrier—out of storage and give it to Kenneth as payment for the three months' rent I owe him. The ankle-length Blackglama mink coat I sell for $1,000 to a friend of David's, a furrier with a shop on Lincoln Road in South Beach. Because I can't imagine myself eating my dog Elmo, I do not eat or wear anything that comes from an animal. I am thrilled that I can give away all the leather shoes and handbags I had saved to the women in the shelter where I volunteer, and give facials and apply their makeup, which I then donate.

* * *

It is Saturday afternoon. We are listening to a live broadcast of *Carmen* from the Metropolitan Opera on the small radio I bring to the nursing home. Rita's eyes are open wide. I wonder if she is remembering all the nights when she sat with Papa in the beautiful opera house in Berlin.

"Our small girl is such a grownup lady! She sits so quietly in her seat. How her eyes open wide when it is *Carmen*, our favorite opera," Papa bragged to his wife, Mali. This is Rita's favorite memory.

I am singing along when suddenly a new doctor walks into Rita's room. I know immediately that God has sent him. He is the one who will set her free. And, like Mama and Rita, he has red hair.

He schedules a meeting with her immediate family to discuss Rita's future.

"It's time to let her go," he urges.

He asks for permission to remove her feeding tube as soon as possible. Her condition will never get better.

"She will not suffer, nor will she die of starvation," the doctor promises us. He recommends placing her in hospice care where no aggressive measures will be taken to keep her alive. She will not feel a moment's discomfort or pain. Her death will take anywhere from four to ten days, and at the very end he will medicate her with morphine. It will look as though she has just gone to sleep. I know that because of this wonderful doctor, we will get Jack to agree to remove the horrid feeding tube. Victory feels so hollow now. My sister was a prisoner in her own body. If her family had only listened to my plea—"Don't do this. Please let her go."—she could have been spared this yearlong violation.

When I arrive the next morning, there is no more tube or needle anywhere in her body. I am finally able to gather Rita in my arms. I get into bed beside her. I cradle my precious sister, my rock, witness to my forgotten early life, my hero, and sob from deep inside of me. "You kept your promise to Mama. You took care of the baby."

Desperate to be in every moment of Rita's soon-to-be-ended life, I come before daybreak, before her family arrives. It's just Rita and me. I concentrate on being there to look at her and to touch her, and to try to let her go. I do not show my anguish at wanting to hold on to her. When I enter her room, her hand reaches into the air like she wants to touch me. Her eyes smile at the sight of me. I curse God for taking her. I thank God for taking her. Wrapping her in a blanket, I lift her onto a special rolling lounge chair and wheel her outside, where she can feel the sun on her face. Her skin glows. Her eyes still open wide. I put another ice cube on her tongue, and as I wait for it to melt my mind wanders back to 1982, the last time I sat with Rita in her Cleveland kitchen.

"It is May 5, 1945. Susi is twelve years old when her teacher announces, "The war is over—you will all go home now." Rita's eyes are moist as she recounts how Susi ran home to her kind Swiss caretakers, the family Brauchly, and telephoned. "Get ready, Rita! Mama and Papa are coming to take us home now."

"Every day I searched for their names on the list of survivors that was pasted on the wall in the Zurich Town Hall, and then I'd run home and look out the window, waiting for our parents to come. With every day that our parents failed to turn up, it felt less that they were still alive. May ended, then June and then July."

And now, five decades later, as I hold her head back and point my finger at the puff of white cloud that has strayed across a powder-blue Miami sky, from her great charm and warmth a beautiful smile floats across her face when I say, "Mama. Papa. Home."

Almost ten days have passed since the tube was removed. I have just finished getting her ready for bed when I feel the need to open the window. Suddenly a beautiful red butterfly lands on the sill. I climb into Rita's bed. I know that soon she will leave us and finally be free. I sob as I hold her, my tears spilling onto her face. Her bruised, tiny body melts in my arms.

Knowing that now she would be allowed to die, I have rehearsed this scene and all the things I want to tell her before she leaves, but I forget them all. In a voice heavy with pain and sorrow, all I can say is, "Thank you for mothering me when I needed you. What a privilege it has been to mother you at a time when you needed me. I was so blessed and grateful to know that even at my most hysterical, rebellious, and desperate self, I felt fully recognized. I always trusted you to love me even when I had not loved myself."

Rita had loved Shirley Temple, a Granny Smith apple in bed, Nivea crème, and white chocolate. She loved Chanel No. 5 but only used it for very special occasions. Rive Gauche cologne was for every day. She swooned over Paul Newman, and loved concerts and picnics in the park. Picnics always included homemade tuna, macaroni, and her famous egg salad. She never put onions in any of the salads when I came along. Her favorite movies were *Bambi* and *Heidi*. She cried from the start to the end of both, no matter how many times she watched them. Her boys could always count on her for the horror movies. She even cried listening to "The Little Drummer Boy," which she loved. But most of all she loved and cherished the family she was devoted to. I had been helpless, forced to see my precious sister lose, cell by cell, everything she loved and everything she was.

As I watch my beloved sister die, I remember an article I'd read that spoke about the lucky ones. These are the people who die in their sleep dreaming about an old lover they once had. I am filled with waves of sorrow for my Rita and rage against a God I love. Why does my sixty-one-year-old sister, whose holiday table was always surrounded not only by family but also by strangers who had nowhere else to go, who never sat in judgment of me or anyone and who taught me grace, not merit such a death?

Rita had held my sad and tragic history and the remnants of my past. She knew me as a child. She told me who I was. Her stories of the scenes of those early years had shaped my memories: the short life I had spent with my parents, our arrest, the camp, the daily cup of rotten tomato soup, and my three-year-old self running after Mama, pleading for her to take me. Mama's swift and sudden deportation—all of it is gone. It's as if the part of the brain that held the first seven years of my childhood memory has been lobotomized.

I will never again see Rita's beautiful, sparkling hazel eyes, framed by that flaming red hair, smile at me. I have lost my staunchest ally. With Rita I always had a place, no matter how lost, or selfish, or needy, or pathetic, or flippant, or ungrateful I was.

Who will care what happens to me now? Who will remember the child I was?

I feel a kind of numb nothingness, a foreign void, knowing that I will never again pick up the phone and hear the joy and love in her voice when she says my name. But I do not dwell on my own heartbreak now: there will be the rest of my life for that. With a heart that will soon break as I imagine my life without her, in the end I say, "You can go, Rita. You can go."

I got the call at five-thirty in the morning. "Rita is dead," Jack cries. December 7, 1993. It's Pearl Harbor Day. How proud Rita would have been to know that she died on the day that the Americans entered the war. Every Veterans Day would find Rita in a cemetery saying "thank you."

But I had missed my chance to be with her in the end. I left her at ten the night before so that I could catch the last of the two buses I took to go home before they stopped running. I had to walk Elmo, who'd been alone all day. I just thought she would wait for me. I feel an agonizing guilt and loss about the timing of that walk, even though a larger part of me believes it was the right ending. I think it is a scene my sister would have approved of. They buried her in the Holocaust survivor section of the cemetery. I did not go to the funeral. I could not bear to see her put in the ground.

When Jack asked David, "Why is your mom not here today?" my son answered, "My mom was there when it mattered."

Only with the autopsy after her death do we discover that Rita had familial spastic paraplegia, a rare and progressive neurological disease that shares the traits of Alzheimer's and Lou Gehrig's disease.

Her daughter reads me the condolence card she got from Rita's hairdresser in Cleveland that said: *Saturday at 2:30 will always be her time.*

I am happy to know that Rita will never know that her two sons have inherited the disease. Their wishes are clear. No feeding tube and no aggressive care will be allowed.

In 2014, I sat down beside her firstborn in his lovely Tampa house and told him it was okay to go. His eyes looked out into the distance at something that no one else could see. Two days later he was gone. He was sixty-one.

On September 11, 2016, I stood by the open coffin of Rita's middle child, a New York lawyer. "You were a warrior, Mark." He was fifty-nine.

CHAPTER THIRTY-TWO

TWO TO TANGO

On January 8, 1994, one month after Rita's death, I move back home to New York. I rent my friend Marlene's dark, furnished apartment in Gramercy Park, a charming, quiet, and secluded corner of Manhattan. I walk through the old familiar neighborhoods, pointing out favorite spots of mine to Rita, who I imagine is looking down at me.

As I exit the subway station near the hotel on Fifth Avenue, where I have a job interview, I slip and fall on the ice. Now there's a hole in my black stretch hose. My six-year-old faded green coat has a huge black spot from the dirty, melted ice. It's nine o'clock and I'm already late for this interview for a job I desperately need.

On this dark, cold, March morning as I wait for the light to change, a FedEx truck bears down the street toward me. I feel a sudden impulse that I will just throw myself under this truck. I am tired. I feel the weight of my grief. Life has become too hard, and I am tired of fighting to live. I do not care what happens to me anymore. As I step off the curb and into the street I hear a voice shout, "Stop!" Embarrassed and frightened, I do not look up or out at the people crossing the street. Instead I quickly turn and run back to my apartment and miss my interview. I feel like I have plunged into a dark hole. I see no light.

With the hope of finding a job I had sent out dozens of resumes, but in the second month of my long-awaited homecoming I find myself crying all the time. Putting on a happy, cheerful face and dressing up to go on interviews has become harder to do. I am just going through the motions while a voice in my head shouts, "You're fifty-four years old and no one will hire you!"

My grief seems to have no bounds. It makes my son David uncomfortable and impatient when I call him in Florida and tell him that all I can do is lie on the sofa, curled up in a fetal position, weeping for my dead sister. I am engulfed in blackness. Is there a time limit on grief? Have I passed it?

I rage against God for taking away so many more years of my sister's life. They were years from my life too! "Rita," I plead. "I'm not strong enough to do this alone. Please help me get through this." The tiny, dark apartment now feels like a coffin, and, too frightened to venture out, I sense that I have dug a sort of grave.

I know I need help but I do not know anyone I can call. But then I remember. There's a number that I called in 1977 when, as a single mother working three jobs a week, I searched for an affordable camp where I could send my nine-year-old son.

"Good morning, UJA-Federation. How may I direct your call?" says the sweet voice on the phone. I say that I am a Holocaust survivor, that everyone I loved is dead, and that I too want to die. "Don't move from there. Promise me you will not do anything rash. I will have someone get right back to you," she says. In less than five minutes the phone rings. "My name is Dr. Milton Wainberg. I am a psychiatrist with Mount Sinai Hospital, a UJA-Federation agency. I am in charge of a new Holocaust survivors group, and I want to help you. Can you come to my office at eight-thirty tomorrow morning?"

"Dr. Wainberg," I sob into the phone, "I have lost everything. Mama and Papa were murdered in Auschwitz. I've just spent four years at the bedside of my beloved sister. I spent the last year helplessly watching her waste away. I am numb. I feel like a living dead person. I have no job. No God. No faith or hope, and no money. I cannot pay you."

Dr. Wainberg gives me his address and says he will see me in the morning.

* * *

We meet in his office at a mental health clinic on upper Fifth Avenue. He has a wide, easy smile; a soft, lyrical voice with just a hint of a Spanish accent; and a handsome, open face. He asks me to have a seat and says he is glad I have come.

I cry through the entire fifty minutes of this first session and yet I manage to share enough for Dr. Wainberg to diagnose me with post-traumatic stress disorder. "You are a hidden child," he explains. "Rita's death has triggered memories of how terrorized and powerless you felt when your mother was shipped away."

"That can't be," I stammer. "How can I be a child in hiding?"

Memory has not been kind to me. It erased my first seven years. All of it! Not just certain things here and there. The absence of my memory, however, has not meant an absence of suffering. In fact, the opposite is true. It is an extra burden because the scars are there, but I don't know how they got there.

My two older sisters had memories of family, traditions, daily life, and smells and sounds of a past. I have no such memories—not even fragments of my shattered life. "You were too young to have secured a life's foundation, too traumatized to experience childhood, and too preoccupied with survival to reflect on its impact," Dr. Wainberg says.

My journey that began in 1969 with my former therapist, Dr. Bob, had only explored the violent abuse at the hands of Aunt Gerdy. I had become numb to my feelings. Creating unhealthy, destructive relationships with men was the only way I'd known I was alive. But that excavation of my past had not gone deep enough or far back enough. This hidden child part of me has never been addressed. I have been crying out for recognition. Longing to look at my fractured past, I am ready and eager to embark on this new journey.

And so we begin, four times a week, at five dollars a session. Dr. Wainberg tries to hypnotize me into remembering those lost years. Scared that I will lose control, I resist.

Four weeks later, Dr. Wainberg suggests, "Let's try just talking. This might feel safer to you. Come sit in this chair." Looking at his face is much more reassuring as I fight hard to retrieve my lost memories of those early years.

"Try to imagine what that day of September 1942 in the internment camp might have been like," Dr. Wainberg asks. I begin to reconstruct the most important scene in my life, until I have it as whole as the story I have always heard from Rita.

The 3 a.m. roll call. Mama comes into our barrack to dress our three thin, lice-bitten young bodies. Mama tells us to stand in the children's line. She is told to bring her meager belongings for the trip to the work camp in the East.

Mama with her red hair, fine bones, and porcelain skin now freckled from the sun shouts out from her place in line, "Go back to the barracks, my sweet girls! I will be back soon!"

My three-year-old arms outstretched, I run to her. "Mama! Mama! Take me with you!"

"Rita, take care of the baby." It is all that she has time to say to my ten-year-old sister before the French guards push her onto the waiting cattle car to Auschwitz.

Oh, Mama, we never said good-bye! My mother was wrenched away from me, unable to respond to my cries. "Mama, take me!" I was left in limbo without her hug or soothing words of love.

Retrieval of any memory of my first seven years is impossible. When I try to remember that day, and the days and years that followed, I cannot find even a scrap of memory. All I remember are the scenes as told to me by Rita. The anguish I suffer at not having any memories of my own is such an injustice. It has stolen a part of my identity and deprived me of an essential part of myself, leaving a gap that seems like a mystery. I lack a piece of myself. It's such a pity for something to just disappear like that. It sometimes feels like I don't belong anywhere, or to anyone. It's as if I had not even been there.

It is not until my sixth month with Dr. Wainberg when I finally do *feel* Mama's ultimate gift of love. Even though Mama knew nothing of the thousands of deportations that would come later—nor could she have ever imagined the Final Solution—while facing a terrifying unknown, she had made a heart-wrenching choice. She had given me life. Fat tears roll down my face as I realize that I have wasted so many years of my life being ungrateful, carrying bags of guilt that I had been spared.

"What you carry, Sylvia is the knowledge that you really have no right to live."

I am stunned by Dr. Wainberg's words. "You had not been allowed to mourn your mother's too-early departure from your young life," he adds. "The guilt and dammed-up sorrow you carry had you squander away so many years trying, but failing, to feel deserving of having lived."

"Mourning provides relief," my doctor says. "When we mourn we excrete the pain, the sadness, the anger, and the guilt. The body and mind are cleansed to re-enter the world refreshed. But, because you had not been allowed to mourn, you remained locked in all that sorrow, pain, and guilt searing your soul.

"Sylvia, you have carried the day your mother left you in Camp Rivesaltes inside you like an embryo. It has left a deep, scarring wound that will never completely heal. I believe that the day your mother left was the moment your life was ripped to shreds. No one was prepared to hear the story that dominated your life. Perhaps because everything of real value had been taken away from you, your early retreat from the pain and horror has carried the seeds of the life you've lived without memory. You were just a child. You did not understand what was going on."

I have acres and miles and years of grief inside of me. I had been evicted from my childhood. The messages of shame and silence had erased my life. Who I was was never good enough. I had no history, so I had to make one up. I had to make me up to survive—which was yet another version of hiding. The real me had disappeared.

"Survivor guilt is the term most commonly used to describe the feelings of those who emerge from a disaster which mortally engulfs others," Dr. Wainberg explains. "On an irrational level these individuals flinch at their privileged escape from death's clutches. But, because of the constraints enforced on you not to express your rage outward, you turned it inward and upon yourself. Guilt is anger directed toward the self. Guilt and shame were the price you were forced to pay for the gift of having survived."

I am overwhelmed by this new insight. I had grown up believing that I had done something bad. That I was bad, and that my history had been so wrong that it had to be erased. I stumbled through life with a fear of abandonment. Rita's early warning—"Be a good girl. Don't make them sad or angry or they will make you leave too."—always echoed in my head. I went through life beginning every sentence with "I'm sorry," and minimizing my own feelings, an all-too-familiar message of silence. Tiptoeing and making myself small because I had to earn the right to stay, I had to earn my life.

I want to explode with a rage so vast that it frightens me. Tears and snot are running down my face and I am unable to speak. It's hard to breathe. Dr. Wainberg brings me a glass of water, and as I reach for the glass, I look into his eyes and I see my sorrow.

"I mourn for that little girl," I cry to him and to myself. "I want to hold her in my arms and beg for forgiveness. I had allowed her to became smaller and smaller until she became invisible. I did not protect her, Dr. Wainberg!"

"Sylvia, the years that you spent at Rita's bedside and the commitment you showed in mothering your sister also helped you to mother yourself. Rita's disease left her with no memory of *who* you were to her—yet she truly knew *what* you were to her.

"As a child you had no voice. As an adult you had become numb, living on the edge; and afraid of the silence, you created drama to feel alive. Aunt Gerdy had held up the mirror that you used to see yourself. Shame and loathing is what it held." It's strange what happens when I hear that name. A trancelike state overtakes me, and the person talking to me fades away; the past becomes more alive than the present. But Dr. Wainberg brings me back when he says, "Rita saw past the damaged and wounded person you had become. She mirrored your true self. The self that is good enough. That has always been good enough."

The rules of Gerdy's strict upbringing had defined me and kept me in place. With the help of my kind and caring therapist, it has taken half my life to cast her rules aside.

"Acknowledge your courage and your strength. Don't be afraid to show how fragile you sometimes feel. And, Sylvia, forgive yourself the years you wasted feeling unworthy of your mother's sacrifice."

I am fifty-five when I am finally allowed to grieve. To feel the loss!

Maybe I will never achieve the kind of success I imagined I needed to be worthy of my mother's sacrifice. But I will try to remind myself that the life she gave me is an extra. It is an unearned gift. All I have to do is breathe. And be grateful. Twelve months from the day I arrived in his office, I sense somehow that my day of liberation has arrived. We know it is time for me to end my therapy.

It is time to truly say *good-bye*. To Rita, to Mama, to Papa, to Milton, to Dr. Wainberg, and to all those I will need to say good-bye to in the years ahead.

Losing Rita will never get easier. It will just change.

Now I commit to living large no matter the danger or the stakes, and to let go of sorrow and shame.

With Dr. Wainberg's wisdom and care, I have come out of hiding. The safety he offered four times a week allowed me to look at a past that had lain on my skin with shame. For the first time I feel a small bubble of pride. What had once been my shame has become my strength.

The butterfly I saw on Rita's windowsill was not only a sign of her freedom, it was a sign of mine. Like the cocoon it once was, the butterfly is like my own freedom—assured only when I share my story and stay out of hiding. My liberation did not happen in 1945 when the war was over—my liberation happened in 1995.

With a hint of tears, Dr. Wainberg reaches for my hand to say good-bye. Instead, I hug him tightly, whispering softly, "Thank you for saving my life."

"I could not have done it if you had not tangoed with me," he says.

It is said that the tango was very popular in the world of Buenos Aires brothels. The young working-class immigrant men who came to Argentina would seek comfort in the drink and the female companionship they found there. The distinguished Argentine author Jorge Luis Borges believed that the tango was born in these brothels. It is quite a performance we see these migrant men do on the dance floor. They have gone through the earthquake of uprooting and personal catastrophes. Every person who survives this uprooting finds himself in exile. Everything has turned upside down, and the world around them is no longer that solid and reliable place where they used to feel comfortable.

Uprooting is a devastating blow because you have to separate yourself overnight from your parents, your language, your country, and your identity. We exiles are not just someone who has lost our home; we are someone who cannot find another. Some of us no longer even know what "home" means.

Survival is inscribed in the dance's movements. The tango is an uncanny mix of vulnerability and strength, Borges wrote.

I am laughing as I remember the fifteen-year-old girl I had once been, and how, during one magical summer in Fleischmanns, New York, another kind and gentle, smiling young man, a child of the Holocaust named Rudy, took a fat, self-loathing, lonely, orphaned refugee and tangoed with her.

CHAPTER THIRTY-THREE

HOW TO SAY GOOD-BYE

It is a cool fall day when I go with my friend Diane to her Narcotics Anonymous meeting. She will share her recovery of one year clean and sober with the group. The meeting is held in a dark, dingy room with a dozen people sitting around a long, old, cigarette-stained wood table. As Diane talks about her life as an addict, my heart breaks for her and my brother Michel. Sometimes the pain in the room is nearly unbearable. Without respite I hear, see, and most of all I *feel* the heart-tearing bleakness of the lives of people who are drug addicts.

I am returned to the moment in 1983 when I had that brief and devastating phone conversation with Michel. It was a dark day during a year of me in pain and grief over my Milton's death. The memory of it still stings. I think about Michel. I miss him so I decide to fly to Los Angeles to visit him.

On a hot and humid July day in 1997, Michel drives me to a quiet, landscaped park in Los Angeles. We have not spoken nor have I seen him since he hurled those ugly words, "I cannot do that," at me. I was mortified by his betrayal. It seemed as if he had not even known me.

He looks healthy and centered and visibly uncomfortable. I am sweating from the heat and anxiety. We make small talk about his ongoing struggle to get back into the theater and all the different projects he's pitched and how they have all failed. He's a salesman at a Nordstrom department store. I hold my breath. I want to cry for him.

Michel knows exactly which dark corner I am now visiting in my mind. The elephant is sitting with us on this bench in this peaceful park. We have been tiptoeing around it for the last hour. At first he brushed past my question, "How could you do that to me?" I swallow hard over the lump in my throat as I wait for Michel to speak.

"I was a drug addict," he says. "I'm sorry I hurt you, but sadly that's what addicts do to people they love. All the money I made from *Nine* went up my nose until I had no more."

It is not quite the apology that I have waited fourteen years to hear. But I know this arrogant and blank-faced Michel. It's a cover-up. He's afraid to show me how frightened and ashamed he really feels. I hold him in my arms, and my body floods with relief. "Michel, I'm so happy that we have begun to find a way back to each other," I whisper in his ear.

How could I have ever imagined at that moment in 1997, in the park with my brother Michel, that three months later he would die from the injuries he sustained while driving home on the beautiful Pacific Coast Highway in Los Angeles? His untimely death is caused by a car crash. He was driving home from the Narcotics Anonymous meeting that he had attended every day for the last ten years. He was fifty-four.

Our brother Stuart has Michel's body shipped to the New Jersey cemetery for burial. Roberta, Michel's friend of forty years, ships a medium-sized box with his meager belongings to Stuart. I take the framed photograph, the black-and-gold mezuzah, and the black glass worry beads that Michel used when he meditated. The simple framed photograph had sat on an easel by a small gold Buddha, behind the burning incense. It looked like a shrine. In the photograph, he is five years old, and although he had removed the other half of the picture, I recognize the hand that rests on Michel's shoulder. It is mine.

I am asked to give the eulogy. I talk about a pajama-clad, tow-haired, three-year-old boy. He had given me a precious gift when his hand had reached out to me, a deeply traumatized, desperately bereaved, seven-year-old orphaned refugee. "Welcome," it said—into his family, his life, and his love.

And, in that magic moment five decades earlier, Michel had won my heart, my loyalty, my gratitude, and my love.

But something died when he refused to return my money and said those ugly words, "I cannot do that." I had been wounded, cast aside, shamed, made invisible by someone I deeply loved and trusted. No longer do I use "Michel Stuart's sister" as my identity. I am forced to go in search of my own authentic self. It is Michel's last gift to me. Today I get back the Michel I'd idolized and loved before it all went bad. Today I get back the simple version. Michel had loved me from the start.

With Milton, Rita, and Michel gone, life gets lonelier.

CHAPTER THIRTY-FOUR

MY GERMAN CONNECTION

Tonight the meeting of the Jewish Child Survivors group I had joined two months earlier will be held in the Park East Synagogue. We usually meet in someone's home, but this group tonight is too big. We have a guest speaker, a professor of German law at a well-known university in New York who has just come out with a new book.

His voice is monotonous, the talk is boring, and I'm nodding off. When I hear him say something about Article 116, 1949, I sit up, wide-awake.

"Former German citizens who were deprived of their citizenship on political, racial, or religious grounds, and their *descendants*, shall on application have their citizenship restored," he says.

It is a cool fall day in 1997 when I walk into the German Embassy in New York to apply for German citizenship. Article 116 is the law that Germany had passed in 1949 to restore to the surviving Jews the German nationality that had been taken from them by Hitler and the Nuremberg Laws. Because they had taken everything—my parents and a life not lived with them in it—retrieving my parents' citizenship has become an obsession and obligation. I'm all they have. I have to have it.

I hope that Christina Brunsch, the kind vice-consul, will be sympathetic and understanding of my need to have something, anything, of my murdered parents. Two years later, Christina calls to tell me that no proof has been found that my father ever had German nationality.

"I'm sorry, but citizenship in Germany is only obtained through *jus sanguinis* (blood rights) from the father, and because your father's father, Markus, was Polish, your father was not a German citizen, even though both sets of your grandparents had lived in Germany since the early 1800s." I am insulted and enraged. I want to scream to Christina: *Even now Jewish blood is not good enough for you Germans. Now I am even more determined—no, I'm committed—to obtaining my parents' citizenship. I will not let go of this. My parents are counting on me.* So I say nothing. I just hang up the phone.

PART III
Found

CHAPTER THIRTY-FIVE

BREAKING THE SILENCE

Now an executive vice-president emeritus of UJA since 1986, my friend Ernie Michel still maintains a small office in the building and remains busier than ever helping people in need. He tells me to write a letter to the new executive vice president of the UJA-Federation.

December 23, 1998

Mr. Stephen Solender

Executive Vice President

UJA-Federation

130 East 59th Street

New York, NY 10022

Dear Mr. Solender,

UJA-Federation has saved another life. Mine!

It was March 4, 1994 when I came back to my beloved New York after the death of my sister Rita two months earlier. She had been like a mother to me. With no money, no job, no friends, no hope, my joy at being back quickly turned to despair. I fell into a deep depression and with no way out I imagined hurling myself in front of an oncoming truck.

With one final desperate plea for help, I called 980-1000.

"Good morning, UJA, how may I help you?" said the cheerful voice on the phone. I said, "My name is Sylvia Ruth Gutmann. I am a Holocaust survivor and everyone I love is gone or dead, and I too want to die." In a worried yet calming voice, the lady, whose name I do not know, made me promise not to do anything rash, and promised to have someone get back to me. In less than five minutes the phone rang, and a gentle voice said, "My name is Dr. Milton Wainberg."

For the next twelve months, four times a week, at five dollars a session, which the UJA provided, Dr. Wainberg and I worked together to help save my life.

Since April 1996 I have had a job at the UJA-funded Federation Employment and Guidance Services (FEGS) as Program Coordinator of the Citizenship Initiative. It is a much-needed program that pairs up our volunteers with seniors from the former Soviet Union who desperately need to learn English in preparation for becoming citizens.

As you can see, I am well on the way back and now I want to *give back*. I would be honored to share with others the story of the life-giving support I received through the UJA.

Most sincerely,

Ms. Sylvia Ruth Gutmann

It is Tuesday afternoon in my office on Hudson Street in Manhattan, where I teach English to two elderly couples, the Daskovs and the Borzakovs. These four Russian immigrants travel an hour and a half from their home in Sheepshead Bay, Brooklyn, for our sessions.

I speak slowly and loudly, and even after Mr. Daskov tells me, "I am partially blind, not deaf," I still do it.

"I am sure that you did not watch American tel-e-vision." I slowly enunciate the homework I give them every week. "I know it is hard for you to watch American shows since Russian is your mother tongue, but it is English you need to learn and television is an easy way to learn it."

But ten weeks later they still look at me as if I speak in Mandarin. At this point I am afraid they will not know enough English to take their American citizenship test.

This week Mrs. Borzakov has brought me her homemade Russian Easter cake, which we eat with coffee I have ordered from the corner store. The telephone rings. With my mouth full of raisins, nuts, cherries, and sweet dough, I answer the phone in a garbled voice, "The Citizenship Program. This is Sylvia. How may I help you?"

"This is Stephen Solender," booms the voice on the phone. "Would you be available sometime this week to come to my office? I need to meet the woman who made me cry."

I clutch the telephone as if it were on fire. My cheeks are filled with cake as I silently point at the tissue box that sits next to the Daskovs' empty paper plates. Mrs. Daskov hands me the plate. "No, no," I silently mouth. I make a gesture with my thumb and index finger like I'm blowing my nose. She hands me the box. I take out a tissue and spit out my cake, but I cannot speak. I am speechless.

I had had no response to my letter for over two months, so I began to think that Mr. Solender was just too busy and that he had no time for me. I wonder what he wants from me now. I have a job I love, but my salary just barely covers all of my expenses. I begin to worry that perhaps he wants me to make a donation to the UJA-Federation, although I don't even have a dollar to spare. I want to show my support for this magnificent not-for-profit global organization by sharing my story and thanking the donors. This is what I hope as I hang silent on the phone.

I have not even noticed that my Russians have fled; yet I am happy that I am alone so that I can concentrate on holding back the tears that are threatening to burst out like a dam. In a sort of whisper-stammer I squeak out to Stephen Solender, the executive VP of the largest local philanthropy organization in the world, "When?... Yes."

One week later I am greeted by a tall, handsome, elegantly dressed man who says, "Please call me Steve." He pulls back the chair in front of his desk, where he motions for me to sit. His eyes are kind. They remind me of my Elmo, the sweet rescued San Diego dachshund that I'd had to put to sleep so many years ago.

"I showed your letter to Mindy, our UJA Speakers Bureau director, and we both feel that your story speaks to what the UJA-Federation is all about. We are in the business of helping all those in need, be they Jews or non-Jews, be it here in America or in Israel or really anywhere in the world. We want you to share your story with our Federation donors of how the UJA has helped you."

On a mild April evening in 1998, six months after that meeting with Steve, I ride with Scott, the event chairman, to the Temple Hillel Annual Donor Dinner in North Woodmere, New York, to my first event as a speaker for the UJA. He knows this is the first time that I will share my story in front of an audience, and he looks a bit nervous about that. I sense that a lot depends on what I can create in that room. "Mindy only told us that you have an incredible story and that you will inspire our donors to donate at the highest level. After I introduce you, you'll have twenty minutes to speak. Could you read me your speech?" asks Scott.

"Huh? I didn't prepare a written speech. I will just share my story of how the UJA helped save my life," I reply.

* * *

I now do two speaking engagements a week, mostly in New York and New Jersey, but eight months later Mindy asks me to come to her office.

"Steve and I agree. We want to put you on the UJA National Speakers Bureau. You will travel throughout the country sharing your story," Mindy says. "The UJA pays your airfare, your transportation to and from the airport, your hotel, your meals, and six hundred dollars per event."

"The Portland Jewish Federation of Portland, Oregon, asked that I not send a high-profile speaker this year," Mindy continues. "Although most of your events have been somewhat small and intimate, and because of the great feedback I always get from the event chairperson, I know that you will touch and inspire the Portland donors too." Mindy hands me my round-trip plane tickets and my Portland itinerary.

* * *

I am standing on the stage of an enormous, softly lit ballroom in the Marriott Hotel in downtown Portland on June 20, 1999.

"I literally would not be alive today if not for the phone calls you make, the donor events that you organize, and the donations that you make. I put a face on all that you do. You make a difference. You save lives," I tell the one thousand Federation donors at the Jewish Federation of Portland thank-you event.

I tell them about how I'd almost hurled myself in front of an oncoming FedEx truck and the voice I'd heard shouting "Stop!" that I believed to be my dead sister. I tell them how a desperate phone call for help was answered by a telephone operator and handled with dignity and compassion. I tell them about Dr. Wainberg, the psychiatrist who normally charges 150 dollars an hour but met with me four times a week at five dollars a session because the study of post-traumatic stress disorder on Holocaust survivors that he headed was funded by the UJA-Federation of New York.

I tell them about being a single mother working three jobs a week, desperate for childcare and unable to afford that care during the long summer months when school was out, and how for a nominal fee they had given my nine-year-old son two months of fun at Surprise Lake, a sleep-away Jewish Federation-funded camp in Cold Springs, New York.

The room is silent. Gold-lined white dinner plates of food are quietly taken away by wait staff that stand in the back of the ballroom and listen with open mouths as I lift the microphone off its stand and step away from the lectern. I stand at the edge of the podium, my eyes looking out at this crowd of people, and I say, "The thirteenth-century German mystic Meister Eckhart said that if the only prayer one ever uttered was 'thank you,' that would be enough." Their eyes are teary and that makes me cry too.

"While I know that the Jewish Federation has helped me here in America, I never knew that the Federation had played a very important life-saving role in my survival during the Holocaust too. The farmhouse in Annemasse, France, where my two sisters and I were taken, had really been a safe house, one of many that had been organized by the *Oeuvre de Secours aux Enfants*, the Organization to Save the Children (OSE). The three men on their bicycles, with milk cans hanging from their shoulders, who smuggled us to the Swiss border, were also organized by the OSE. The OSE saved six thousand Jewish children, including my two sisters and me, from certain death at the hands of the Vichy police and the Nazi SS. The American Joint Distribution Committee funded the OSE, and you know who funds the 'Joint.' It was then, as it is now, funded by the United Jewish Federations."

I am pictured in the *Oregon Jewish Review* embracing Henry B., a Jewish leader. He called my story the most moving of any Jewish Federation of Portland event he ever attended. "That which is spoken from the heart is heard by the heart and the reason we have raised a half a million dollars tonight," he said.

After a lifelong silence during which I had become invisible, I have remarkably and unexpectedly become a sought-after speaker. Each time I share my story, the experience brings me closer to the family I lost. I give them faces and voices. I give them a life they did not get to live.

My audiences are left with an indelible imprint on their souls. I am left more healed, with my wound no longer openly festering.

In September 1999, I receive a short letter that moves me to tears.

Dear Sylvia,

I am so happy for you. It sounds like you have found exactly your place.

Even though you might feel like a wanderer, I think you carry *home* with you to each of your presentations.

So you are your own *home* wherever you are! Congratulations!

Milton L. Wainberg, MD

CHAPTER THIRTY-SIX

LONG AGO AND FAR AWAY

At a Federation event in Maryland, where I am the guest speaker, I meet Irene. "I was very moved by your story. Have you ever thought about writing a book?" This is not the first time someone has floated this suggestion. With no knowledge of computers, which feel to me like the equivalent of climbing Mount Everest, I confess to her that I am even afraid to learn how to use one.

"I could help you with that," Irene offers. "I would do a series of interviews with you. You would only have to speak into my tape recorder. I'd listen to the tape and type it onto my computer. Then I will print out the interviews and bring them to you. Those pages could become your book."

* * *

A month later, she says, "I did a search on the Internet. You have talked so often of the village Nay in France as the last place you lived with your family, and of Madame Bouhot and her daughter Madeleine. There are two Bouhots living in Nay. If you write a letter I will gladly translate it into French. I still remember most of my high school French, and my friend Cosette has also offered to help me."

Together we compose the following letter:

August 1999

Dear Madeleine,

I am the daughter of Malcha and Nathan Gutmann. My name was Silvie Gutmann when my family rented a room in your home during 1941-42. In August of 1942, the French police arrested my mother, my two older sisters, Rita and Susi and me.

My parents were murdered in Auschwitz.

In this letter, I have enclosed a photograph of me with my parents. I look to be about two and a half years old. Now I too am a mother. My son David is thirty-two years old.

I hope to hear from you. I send along my sincere sentiments.

Sincerely,

Sylvia Ruth Gutmann

* * *

September 1999

Madame Madeleine Cance-Bouhot
H7 Cote St. Martin
66800 Nay, France

Dear Silvie,

My cousin Odette Bouhot gave me just today your letter of August 29. I was pleasantly surprised to receive your letter after so many years. I recall very well all of your family. I was at that time thirteen years old and I lived with my mother. I recognize very well from the photo you sent me your Mama, your Papa, your two sisters, and you as well. You were a beautiful little girl.

But your story is not altogether accurate. I will tell you the story I know. Your parents lived in my home with their three children—Rita, 10, Susi, 9, and little Silvie, who was only 3. I have never forgotten the day the Gendarmes came to look for only your Mama. Your Papa remained with his three children at the house because he was sick. Your Mama was in tears and despairing of leaving you, but she was forced to depart and was taken to the camp of Rivesaltes in the south of France, then to Auschwitz.

There was then a Jewish committee that took care of you. Your papa was sick and went alone about twenty kilometers toward the mountains into a sanatorium in Eaux-Bonnes where he could rest. Several months later he was arrested and deported to Auschwitz.

You and Susi remained for a short time at our home with my mother and me, who cared for you. Rita was with a neighbor across the street. Finally, the Jewish committee decided to have all three of you leave for Switzerland and thereafter to the United States.

I recall very well having accompanied you with my mother to the station in Nay to put you on the train. I recall all of this very well. I never thought I would ever hear from you again after almost sixty years.

In 1976, I had the surprise one evening of seeing in front of my house your sister Rita and her husband. She remembered the address and she wished to see the house. My mother left the house to me when she died and I live here with Raymond, my husband of fifty years. My three children are grown and no longer live here.

I would love to see you again. Then I can receive you at my house; the house where you last lived with your parents.

Thank you for your letter. I embrace you.

Madeleine

* * *

Dear Madeleine,

Thank you very much for your quick response to my letter. I cannot believe that I am going to see you in the house where my family was last together. I have much to tell you about all that happened to us during the war. The French and German documents that I have received clearly show that sadly, it is your story that is inaccurate.

We three girls were taken with our mother to Rivesaltes, the French internment camp. Rita has shared that day with me so many times: the buses waiting on the corner; the French police; the train that carried the Jews, with black cloth-covered windows in each car, which brought us to the camp. Rita remembered a Mademoiselle Rothschild coming to the camp after Mama was deported. She brought us back to Papa in Eaux-Bonnes. He was very sick and also in danger and could not keep us. Mademoiselle then brought us back to Nay, when Susi and I did stay with you.

After a long and horrible illness my beloved sister Rita died in 1993 at the age of sixty-one. I miss her very much. She was a witness to the early years of my life. I do not have my own memories of that time.

You are a witness too. I hope you will tell me of your memories.

I do not speak French but my friend Irene will be with me to translate.

I am looking forward to seeing you once again.

Lovingly,

Sylvia Ruth Gutmann

CHAPTER THIRTY-SEVEN

BACK TO BEFORE

Irene has paid for our round-trip airfare to Paris, our two-day stay in a small bed and breakfast, our meals, and the train that will take us to Nay, where she has arranged with Madeleine and her husband Raymond to pick us up at the station.

We are standing on the platform of the station in Nay, where a finely dressed elderly couple is walking toward me. He is tall, lean, handsome, and white-haired, and his seventy-six-year-old wife has tightly curled, lacquered brown hair. She is wearing sunglasses and a harlequin-checkered dress. "You look like the same beautiful girl," she says in French.

I begin to cry. This moment is unreal. I am in shock. Shut down. Madeleine looks uncomfortable and embarrassed with my tears; I sense she is not the touchy-feely type like me. So she quickly leads me to the car for the ten-minute drive to the house in Nay.

My mind is blank when I stand in the driveway and see the house: this two-story gray stone house was the last place where I lived with my family. I am clearly not myself, and I'm having a difficult time when Irene translates for me Madeleine's fast-paced French dialogue. "Is the house familiar to you, Silvie?"

"No," I silently mouth.

"It was a very hard time for all of us back then," Madeleine begins. "I remember the ration tickets and how much I missed my butter, which was in very short supply."

I look away and roll my eyes at Irene, who has just translated Madeleine's words. I feel that Madeleine means well, but what a foolish thing to say. My mind wanders away from the translation of Madeleine's words when I realize, again, how the lack of memory during this time shaped my entire life.

Madeleine, Irene, and I are standing in front of a closed door on the top floor of the house. Madeleine takes hold of my hand. I am touched by this show of affection. "This was the room of your family. The fireplace where your mother cooked and heated the water for your bath was removed when my daughters shared this room."

I am looking into the room where I lived with a family, *my family*, and suddenly, the floor feels like it is slipping away. My heart starts doing double time. An ice-cold current creeps down my neck and arms and through my hand, which is clutching onto Madeleine to keep me from falling.

"My mother and I lived on the ground floor," Madeleine continues. "The only way my mother allowed your family to come in and out of this room was by using the staircase that was then outside of the house. The steps were very high, and when your two older sisters were not there and you had to go to the outhouse, you stood at the top of the stairs, a happy, chubby three-year-old crying for 'Malene' to carry you down."

I cannot stretch my mind around this moment. I am stalled in the past. Madeleine has just shown me traces of myself that I do not remember. My sobbing is so loud that I barely hear

Irene when she translates Madeleine's words. "Would you like to sleep in this room tonight?"

Sleep is impossible, and instead of the comfort and peace that I imagined in the very room that had once housed a loving father and mother, my two sisters, and me, I am ill at ease. When I try to picture my parents—my thirty-three-year-old mother, bright red hair beautifully coiffed, elegantly dressed, pretending that all is well, and my forty-year-old Papa suffering with asthma and bedridden—all I see is their fear and despair.

I walk over to the window, and when I open the shutters I see in the distance of the early-morning light the French Pyrenees Mountains. I know that Papa had chosen this little village in the Pyrenees because the SS did not yet occupy it. It was still the "Free Zone," and he'd heard that we could hire a *passeur* to help us cross over the mountains safely into Franco's Spain. I feel waves of grief and anger when I see how close the mountains are. I remember the heartbreaking story of the *passeur*, a local mountain guide who knew the old contraband trails and who was smuggling Jews, who had taken Papa's money but then refused to take us, claiming that I was too young to make such a dangerous journey, and yet he had kept the money anyway.

Hitler had stripped the Jews of their German citizenship by that time so my parents had no papers, which meant they had no work, and little money. All the while they were being hunted and haunted. I think about and marvel at the courage, the ingenuity, and intelligence my parents demonstrated in making our life seem normal as they tried to always stay one step ahead of the Nazi killing machine.

* * *

The following morning I stand in the park that sits at the bottom of the hill from Madeleine and Raymond's house. Raymond has told me that he believes he has found the exact spot by the fence from the 1941 photo I had sent with my first letter to Madeleine. In this photo my mother is holding my hand and my father has his hands wrapped around my shoulders. It looks as if he is holding me up to keep me from falling. Irene, Raymond, Madeleine, and I are the only people in the park, yet I can hear a child laughing and calling for her papa. I see them running around a fountain in my mind. "Madeleine, did there used to be a fountain here? Did I play in this park?" I ask.

"Yes. Your papa used to bring you here. Your mama would pretend to be angry as she gently scolded him for letting you play with the water in the fountain and bringing you home with your hair, your dress, and even your shoes all wet."

I hold my breath. I have just had a real memory. This is not a story that was ever told to me by my sister Rita. I have never heard anything about this park before. A distant memory had been wrangled free from the childhood I don't remember, a kind of greeting from across a half-century.

"Come, Sylvie, now we will drive to Eaux-Bonnes. It is not so far away," says Raymond. I walk through the old sanatorium where my papa had hid and where he signed the papers for the woman on the committee who would secure the rescue of his three precious daughters. It had been a lovely, small hotel after the war, but now it stands empty and desolate. Here I take out a letter from its plastic wrapping, the tiny, fragile, redlined, yellowed letter, written with pencil in German. It is a letter from Papa, a precious gift that I received from my Swiss cousin, Uriel Gast. Papa had written it more than six decades earlier to his nephew Herman, who was Papa's sister Rosa's son and Uriel's great-grandfather.

October 21, 1942 Eaux Bonnes

Dear Herman and Jenny,

I received your card as well as the newspapers with thanks. Now dear Herman I would like a good advice from you and it concerns, as you know my children. They are in Nay in very good hands. They have visited me this week and they look very good. I had great joy with them. The woman cried when I suggested that my children be smuggled into Switzerland. Many here are telling me not to be sentimental and to send them away. Since one does not know what the morning will bring I am not safe here either. My children could be without a father one day and then what?

The committee will provide a person who will bring the children to the border. I ask you now, what shall I do? Can you take the children 100%? My beloved girls have already lost their mother and I am afraid they may also lose their father. I have written to your mother, my sister Rosa, but why have I not had any word from her?

Dear Herman, please can you help my precious girls?

Their safety lies heavy on my heart.

What can I do? Without their father what will happen to my children?

Your Nathan
Maison Cadeux Eaux Bonnes

Four months after he sent this letter to Switzerland, my forty-two-year-old father was arrested by the French Vichy police and deported to Auschwitz, just as his young wife had been five months earlier. This German letter, written by a bedridden, desperate man, a plea to the son of his oldest sister, was never answered.

* * *

This journey back into my past is almost over, but there is one more place I must visit. I am walking up and down the platform of the train station in Nay. Here is where thirteen-year-old Madeleine and her mother had taken their three young charges to meet "the woman" from the committee in Papa's letter. Mademoiselle Rothschild had rescued us from the camp and brought us back for a short time to Nay. Papa had secured her before his arrest when she promised him that she would try to get us safely into Switzerland. Madeleine has recollected some of these early scenes for me.

Over a breakfast of croissants, cheese, and homemade strawberry preserves, Raymond hands me a gray, faux-leather covered picture album. "I made this for you last night while you slept. It is your past in pictures." I open to a map of the Pyrénées-Atlantiques. Raymond has highlighted Pau (the first village where we lived), then circled Nay and Eaux-Bonnes in orange. He has also put together a large sheet of paper with copied photographs.

"This is the house where the Rothschilds lived," Raymond points out. "That is the old *lavoir* where your mama washed the family's clothes. Here is a picture of Rita Rothschild posing next to a twenty-year-old Joujou, her best friend."

I gasp when I see the 1943 color photo of my rescuer, nineteen-year-old Rita Rothschild. She is so beautiful. "Raymond, Madeleine," I beg. "Is she alive?"

"She and her family left here soon after that picture was taken and we lost contact," Madeleine sadly replies.

I am sleep-deprived, drained, and spent. I feel as if I have cried the tears of a whole lifetime and that there are none left. Raymond has put our suitcases into the car. He will drive us to the station in Nay, where a train will take us to Perpignan; the train does not stop in Rivesaltes. Irene will rent a car for the twenty-minute drive. Just as I am about to leave, Madeleine puts an envelope in my hand. She says something in French but Irene is already in the car, and I do not understand. I want to open the envelope but her hands gently sweep me out the door as she says something about Raymond—maybe that he is waiting.

When I open the envelope, more tears come. It is my late sister Rita's handwriting, wishing Madeleine and Raymond a joyous Christmas and signed, *"Je vous embrasse bien Rita, bonjour de Suzi et Sylvie."* An avalanche of emotion pours over me. I wish Rita were here.

I am standing among the ruins in southern France, fifty-six years to the day that my beautiful mother was deported to Auschwitz, leaving me here in Camp Rivesaltes. Etched in my mind is the story of that day. It haunts me still. It will always remain an abject wound that will never heal. It will be with me wherever I go. From this military training camp, the French police shipped 2,500 Jewish men, women, and children to Auschwitz. It sits on a large, desolate plain where the wind blows through what remains of the former barracks.

Only a small roadside marker remains, no taller than I would have been at age three. The only indication a visitor has about its shameful past.

CHAPTER THIRTY-EIGHT

HERO IN CHANEL

I am back at work, jet-lagged, and in the afterglow of the trip that Irene had planned and paid for. A trip I could never have made without her.

I am more determined than ever to find Mademoiselle Rothschild, when I get a letter from Monique, Madeleine's daughter, written in English at Madeleine's request.

Dear Sylvie,

There are 25 days since you came back to N.Y. I was so happy to see you again. It seemed to me I became younger. What memories we had together! I was sad when I learned that you and your sisters had gone to the camp with your brave Mama. I did not remember it that way. I never knew what had happened after my mother and I took you and your two sisters to meet the *lady* on the train so long ago.

I send some photos of our visit for you and for Susi, who is also in my heart, as is Rita… I also send an old address in Paris for Rita Rothschild.

The watch you gave me is OK. I think of you each time I watch the clock. I hope to see you again.

I kiss you tenderly,

Madeleine

* * *

"I have never forgiven Madeleine," Susi said bitterly when I told her that I was planning to visit Madeleine in Nay. "When Papa sent us back to Nay and the Bouhots, Madeleine was wearing Mama's dress. It is one thing to use the objects that had once belonged to my dead mother, but quite another to wear her clothes."

I'm angry and hurt. Whenever Susi shares a family memory, it is her mama, her papa. With Rita, it was our mama, our papa. Susi makes me feel like an outsider. I feel like a needy imposter, so desperate to be included in her family. No, I will not show Susi the pictures, nor will I share the album that Raymond so lovingly made for me.

Hoping to find Mademoiselle Rothschild alive, I send a letter to the address Madeleine had given me. Irene translates my letter to French. "I know it would be a miracle if you were the woman who saved my two sisters and me fifty-seven years ago," I write. "If you are the Mademoiselle of so long ago, I hope that you will let me know this so that I may write you of my profound gratitude."

After two months, I give up hope of finding her. But late one night I open my mailbox and see an envelope with a Paris return address. It is too late to call Irene, so I must wait until morning when the Kinko's copy center opens. They will scan Mademoiselle's letter and then send it to Irene's email address. It feels like forever until Kinko's opens at nine.

"Yes, I am the Mademoiselle with whom you were left so long ago. I only did my duty and am content to know that you have been in good health. If you ever come to Europe, let me know. I will be very happy to meet you."

A woman who writes *I was only doing my duty* is a remarkable human being, I think.

I must meet her. I have no money to make a trip to Paris, but then I remember how the letter I'd written fifteen years earlier had gotten the tuition money for my son's senior year of high school, so I write to *Newsday*, *The New York Times*, and the *New York Post*. I'm pretty confident that *The New York Times* with its Jewish publisher and *Newsday* with their huge Jewish readership on Long Island and Queens will be happy to take part in this profoundly moving story. I'm pretty sure I won't be hearing from the *New York Post*. I do love the gossip on page six, but I don't see a lot of Jewish-sounding names in the staff directory.

In the letter I write: "We have so many stories of dirty politicians, of crime and rape and violence. Do you not wish to tell the story of the nineteen-year-old woman who risked everything to rescue me and my two sisters from a French internment camp in 1942, after my mother had been deported and murdered in Auschwitz?"

The New York Times sends me a form letter that says, "Very moving story, but not for us."

Newsday's response is another variation on that theme.

The paper I had written off as "not Jewish enough," its pages filled with stories of shootings, rapes, child abuse, and celebrity gossip (that I secretly read), called to say, "This is just the kind of story that our chairman and publisher Rupert Murdoch loves."

January 22, 2000

Agreement, between Sylvia Ruth Gutmann and the *New York Post.*

In exchange for an exclusive front-page article about her reunion with the French woman who rescued her from an internment camp, the *Post* has agreed to provide her a first-class, round-trip ticket from New York to Paris with hotel accommodations in the Concorde La Fayette for two nights in Paris. In addition the *Post* will pay for a *New York Post* journalist to accompany her to a reunion dinner at one of Paris' finest restaurants.

Signed,
Senior Editor
New York Post

* * *

Two months later, Uri Dan is waiting for me in the baggage claim of the Charles de Gaulle airport in Paris. Like the limousine drivers that wait holding large white cards with the names of their customers, Uri also holds a card with my name on it. He does not know what I look like, but I recognize him immediately. He looks younger and more handsome than he does in the picture that heads his weekly *Post* political column. Known for his dispatches in the *Post*, he has been the Israel correspondent for the last twenty-five years. Several years ago Uri lived and worked in the *Post*'s Paris bureau. He speaks French like a native. I like him. He is warm and friendly and a take-charge man. I know I am in good hands. All will go well.

"Come, I have a taxi waiting to take us to the hotel. You can freshen up after that long evening flight. We will meet Rita later today." My cheeks are shiny with tears. My rescuer is named Rita. How serendipitous, I think. My late sister Rita's unconditional love rescued me too, in a way. Hers was a rescue of my soul—not only when I was young, but throughout my life, and even now.

After breakfast, a shower, and a makeup refresh, I leave with Uri to Drancy, a Paris suburb that is a forty-five-minute taxi ride away.

I stand with Uri in front of a large, U-shaped white stone apartment complex. A quiet green park in a dreary working-class, mixed-immigrant French suburb surrounds the buildings. There is a railroad track where I walk and approach a boxcar. This is the memorial site of the transit camp Drancy. "The antechamber and waiting room of Auschwitz," says Uri.

In 1941 this was a large, oval complex of unfinished apartment buildings where the French police, under the authority of the Nazi regime, held and then transferred 67,000 captured French and foreign-born Jews. Children were immediately separated from their parents and deported to the death camps. Without care or enough food, and from the brutality of the French guards, the babies and the very young died after arrival. The remaining six thousand children were transported to and gassed in Auschwitz.

The first transport that had been shipped from Camp Rivesaltes to Drancy left for Auschwitz on June 22, 1942. Three months later, convoy #33 carried 586 males and 407 females, most of whom were between the ages of forty and fifty-five. Among them were Poles, Germans, and Austrians who had been surrendered by Vichy and transferred first to Camp Rivesaltes and then to Drancy. SS Rothke, the head of the anti-Jewish section of the Gestapo, wrote on an onionskin list that the train of September 16 departed Drancy with 650 foreign Jews, including my mother, Mali. They arrived in Auschwitz four days later, where 147 women were selected for work. Numbers from 19980 through 20126 were tattooed on their arms. Two hundred able-bodied men were selected for work and also tattooed with numbers. The rest of the convoy, made up of old people, unaccompanied children, and the men and women not selected for work like my mother were immediately gassed.

The following February, convoy #47, carrying my father Nathan, was also en route to Auschwitz.

"Uri, what does the writing on the boxcar say?"

"This sign on the boxcar door says that the car holds eight horses."

This windowless wagon, with no food or water and a single bucket used as a toilet, is where a hundred men, women, and children were piled in for their transport to Auschwitz, a four-day ride away. I am gasping for air.

"This sign shows a Jewish star," Uri adds.

I am frozen and I don't know what to do, so I bang my head on the boxcar door. I need to feel pain. It feels like an insult to the sixty-four transports—carrying some 1,500 people that left for the death camps in a locked airless boxcar like this one—that I am allowed to feel the wind blowing on my face. That I am free to leave from here holding Uri's hand and ride back to my luxurious hotel room. I am clawing, desperately trying to slide open the heavy wooden door and go inside. Maybe I can still summon my parents' smell in the wood, but the door is locked.

* * *

We are told to sit and wait. "She is busy helping a client," says the receptionist at The Service, Rita Rothschild's travel agency. Uri and I are taking her out for lunch and I cannot sit still. I'm nervous but excited too, and so I stand in the hall and wait.

After what feels like hours but is probably no more than ten minutes, a door opens. She is wearing a Chanel suit. Uri stands to greet her in French while I clutch the wall, having lost control. I know I'm too emotional. I've always been that way, and despite my embarrassment and shame, I am sobbing once again.

"Don't cry. Why are you crying?" Rita asks. I can barely breathe or speak when she adds in perfect English, "Look out the window. The sun is shining. It is a beautiful day."

It feels like a dream, like I am not really here. And without knowing how it happened, I am suddenly holding her in my arms.

"You saved my life. You saved my life," I whisper over and over and over again.

"It's nothing," she says, moving toward the front door as if to escape the force of my gratitude.

We are sitting in La Closerie des Lilas on the Boulevard du Montparnasse. "Tourists don't come here," Uri brags. I know the food will be wonderful but Drancy has filled me with so much guilt about being alive and free to eat. The restaurant is warm, inviting, and rich in color with red chairs and a shiny, gorgeous mahogany bar. The lighting is soft and low.

I have no appetite and use my fork to move the fish I've ordered around my plate. I wait until Rita and Uri finish and the staff has cleared the table before I reach into my bag for the small black-and-white photograph—of Mama, Papa, ten-year-old Rita, nine-year-old Susi, and me at age three. It was taken in the family Bouhot's garden in 1942, one week before Mama and her three girls were arrested and shipped to Camp Rivesaltes.

I show it to Rita. I point to my two sisters and me. I want her to say, "Yes, I remember you three. I took you out of the camp and brought you back to your father in Eaux-Bonnes, but he was very ill. I promised him that I would help smuggle you into Switzerland."

But she makes no comment at all, no expression of recognition. Instead she acts as if she had never even heard of us.

When I show her the picture of my thirty-one-year-old son David and tell her, "You gave me a future," a huge smile breaks out across her face. She grabs my hand and shakes it, as if to say "good job."

It is clear from the start that most of my questions will not be answered. I will try again tomorrow.

***

At our farewell dinner she wears a large gold ring, pearls, and another even more stunning Chanel suit accompanied by a Chanel bag. We are seated in Uri's favorite restaurant in the Latin Quarter for our *Post* front-page reunion.

"My father moved his wife, my brother, and me from our home in Cologne, Germany, to Paris in 1933, several months after Hitler came into power," Rita begins. "Six years later, I was sent to an internment camp for German-Jewish aliens. Several months later I was sent to Camp Gurs in the Pyrenees, where my mother would also join me. We lived in the most atrocious conditions, but when the German Nazis approached the Vichy regime, my mother and I were freed. We were reunited with my father and brother and went to work on a farm in Nay. There, I began to work for the Red Cross in 1939, after befriending the dying daughter of an official with the organization. I also became friendly with the Vichy prefect of the region. After Hitler and his German troops marched into Paris on June 14, 1940, and France surrendered, I helped the Vichy prefect find a convent in Lourdes where his Jewish in-laws were in hiding, hoping to survive the war. In return, he gave me false identification papers showing me as a Christian. He also gave me the false papers I needed to help save the Jewish children who were being rounded up and sent to internment camps.

"I remembered the terrible months I had spent in that internment camp, and I knew that now it was even worse. There were at least three transports (to the death camps) a week, and in 1942 I decided in the name of the Red Cross that I would begin to save the children. I brought the children that were left behind by deported parents to the farmers living in the area. I was nineteen years old."

She is quiet and stoic, but still I press her to tell me how she managed to take the children out of the camp, and just for a tiny moment I see a look of pain on her face, but she does not answer me.

"I saved so many children that I don't remember anything about you or your sisters. For so many years I had nightmares, and I would wake up crying because of what I had lived through. I don't wish to relive the frightening, dangerous days I spent smuggling children to safety or my escape to Spain after the German and Vichy police caught on to my illegal rescue operation in 1944. It belongs to the past."

She has Uri promise her that when he writes the article he will refer to her only as *Mademoiselle* Rothschild and that her married name not be published. "I have turned the page. I want to forget all those horrible things. I live in another world today."

"No, no," Rita demands when Uri asks to take a picture of Rita and me. "Not my face, Monsieur Uri. You will not show my face."

As we leave, I stand up and pull her gently into my arms. "Your mother was a brave woman to leave you and your sisters in Rivesaltes," Rita whispers.

"Thank you for saving my life. I live it not only for me, but also for you, for Mama and Papa, and for my sister Rita too."

As I fly home from my two-day visit in Paris I think about my parents. I feel the chaos, the stress, and the fear—because, along with the running and trying to stay away from the killing machines, they did not speak French. They were strangers in a strange land, fighting to survive, as I would be in New York City.

CHAPTER THIRTY-NINE

UP CLOSE AND EVIL

In 2001, I am asked to be part of a weeklong leadership program called the March of Remembrance and Hope. This global project will bring together survivors of the Holocaust with university students of various religious and ethnic backgrounds from North America and Europe to show them the dangers of intolerance and indifference in creating genocides. Program participants will study the Holocaust by visiting the death camps of Poland.

On the night before my visit, I dream about my parents. I dream that they had been waiting for me. "What took you so long?" they say after I rush into their open arms.

Today it is a beautiful May morning, not a cloud in the sky, when I stand on a makeshift stage by the burnt-out shell of what remains of Crematorium 4 in Auschwitz. "This is sacred ground. Here lie the scattered ashes of my parents and the thousands of men and women and children who perished here," I shout to the more than four hundred university students who are here with me.

The students have left and I stand alone on the stage with my grief as I watch him walk toward me. A fancy camera hangs from his neck and his dark, curly hair bounces with each step.

"I am here with my German Holocaust studies class," he says. "They asked that I take pictures of this important event, but I could not aim because my tears were dripping onto the lens."

I have never seen eyes that so perfectly match the color of a shirt. Blue looks out at me. I want to swim naked in his eyes. I suck in my breath and lower my head because I don't want him to see the blush that I feel creeping up from my neck to my face. I hear a rushing in my ears, my breathing is labored, and although I can hear his voice it sounds as if I am underwater. I study him as he speaks—his innocence, his enthusiasm, and his curiosity. He is so beautiful. I feel butterflies flapping in my stomach. Afraid that my shortness of breath is a sign of overheating, he offers me a drink from his half-empty bottle of water. I shiver from the thrill of having my lips touch the same spot as his did.

"My name is Jannek," he whispers. "My father is also Jannek. It is a very common Czech name." He studied the German language, speaks like a native, and is enrolled in a prestigious German university in Munich. "I am only twenty-two and the smartest man in my undergraduate program," he brags. That he has used the word "man" has not been lost on me, a woman forty years his senior.

I am slow and somber as I walk to the bus that will take us back to the Krakow hotel when I see Jannek's German professor sitting alone on the railroad track. It is the track in front of the *Arbeit Macht Frei* sign. And, so softly I can barely hear him, avoiding eye contact, and looking out at the miles of barbed wire that surrounds the rows and rows of barracks in this gruesome place, the professor asks, "Will you share your story of survival in the hotel tonight?"

I want to run away from him. How can he ask me to do this? I have only shared my story in America. Just the sound of a German accent freezes me with fear. *They are murderers and Jew haters.* And yet, I sense that this is an omen, a sign from God.

I know that the Holocaust and its aftermath cannot be fully understood unless it is viewed through the eyes of someone who has lived through it. To speak of it as merely "six million" dehumanizes the victims and trivializes the profoundly human tragedy that it was. I know in my heart that not only is my story worth telling, but that by sharing it with these young people I will finally put a face on what they've only seen in the movies, or on television, or in their textbooks.

I see a hundred students, sitting in a circle, on ugly brown wooden chairs when I open the hotel ballroom door. I walk to the center of the room. The American and Canadian groups surround me on my left. To my right sit the German, the Danish, the Polish, the Japanese, and the Israeli groups. I recognize the two German men sitting in the first row. I had noticed them, whispering and pointing at me, from that makeshift stage by Crematorium 4 where I spoke earlier in the day. They are slouched in their chairs, their legs spread wide apart, their arms crossed. Threatening, defiant, and arrogant is what their body language tells me. A shiver of fear goes through my body. I will play it safe. "Will someone share with us how you felt after our visit in Auschwitz today?" I say.

A young woman in the last row has raised her arm. I ask her to stand. I wait for her to speak.

"I was waiting for the bus that would take me and my class back to the hotel in Krakow," she says in German-accented

English. "A group of American students just walked past me, headed for their buses too. I did not respond when they smiled and said hello. I could not let them hear my German accent. I was so ashamed of what I had seen in the camp, the inhumanity of man, of the German people, my people." The room gets still. Jannek puts his camera down. The two German men sit up straight and uncross their arms. I walk to her side and gather her quivering body in my arms and, with tear-soaked cheek pressed against tear-soaked cheek, she whispers, "Forgive me."

"There is nothing to forgive," I reply. "You have done nothing."

What I have encountered tonight is their guilt and shame. The weight of the Holocaust has burdened them too.

* * *

On the last day of this weeklong leadership program, the eight buses full of students and teachers visit the Treblinka death camp. As part of Operation Reinhard, the Nazi authorities chose to locate this killing center in a sparsely populated area near the village of Treblinka, because it was heavily wooded and hidden from view. The incoming trains of about fifty or sixty cars, filled with their human cargo, arrived at the Ober Majdan station (the real Polish town was four miles away), a disguise for the crematoriums it hid. Complete with made-up train schedules, a fake train station clock with painted-on hands, and a fake ticket window, the people were told that this was to be their new home. Here in Treblinka, we are told to wander alone, unlike when we visited Auschwitz, Majdanek, Belzec, and Plaszow (the labor camp made famous in the film *Schindler's List*), where we stayed in groups, always with a Polish guide, a mental health professional, and a Holocaust survivor like me.

At the entrance to the former camp, our Polish bus driver hands me an information pamphlet that says, "In the relatively short time of its existence this camp took the lives of more than 850,000 Jewish men, women, and children." I am feeling uneasy and anxious as I walk to the site of the former camp. It's a brilliant blue-sky day. The air is still and the birds are singing when suddenly, all my eyes can see are hundreds of large stone tablets reaching up from a concrete-covered field. They look like tombstones, but as I get closer I see that on each tablet is written the name of a once-thriving village that is no more. There are no barracks. No ovens or places of torture. No gas chambers and no crematoriums here. Before shutting down this death camp the Nazis destroyed all the evidence of their atrocities and the ground was plowed and planted over. These rocks, like jagged wounds, are the only witnesses to the hundreds of men, women, and children of those vanished villages, all of whom perished in this camp.

I feel nauseous and lightheaded when I read the plaque hanging alongside the huge black hole in the field where I stand. It says that this is the pyre where the guards had thrown and burned hundreds of living children before they fled the arrival of the Allied troops. This is too much evil; I cannot breathe. There is a terrible pain in my chest and I stand frozen, unable to scream or cry. I fall to my knees and do not hear Jannek approach. He does not speak as he takes up my hand, kisses it, and holds it to his lips and then his cheek. I do not move or pull away, not even when my fingers are wet from his tears.

Breakfast is at dawn. The Canadians and Americans have early-morning flights, unlike the Europeans, who will leave later in the day. I am sad that I did not say good-bye to Jannek at the camp the day before, but just as I am about to board the bus for the airport, I see him running toward me, pencil and paper in hand, wearing the light-blue shirt that matches his eyes, and a smile so beautiful that I feel my heart lurch. He is shouting, "Give me your number, please!" and just as I am about to reach the last step before I take my seat, he whispers, "I am a Jew, too."

CHAPTER FORTY

LOVE AND OTHER DIFFICULTIES

I am back in my dark, two-room apartment on the Upper West Side where my friend who had been watering my plants is waiting for me. Even before I have set my suitcase down, before I can answer the ringing telephone, before I take my jacket off, and even without her glasses on, Jean shouts, "You're in love!"

I pick up the telephone on the fifth ring and I hear him say, "Hello. I am Jannek. I spoke to my political science professor about having you come and speak to the entire student body. We don't have many survivors in Munich who wish to speak about their experiences and their life after the war. Please, will you come?"

"Oh, my God, it's him," I silently mouth to my smiling friend.

"Look at you, all red in the face like some silly teenager with her first crush!" she whispers back.

"Jannek," I answer. "I cannot come to Germany. It's one thing for me to have spoken that evening after Auschwitz at the Krakow hotel. It felt safe because of the hundred students sitting in the room that night; half of them were American. For me to be in Germany, that I cannot do. No, no, I will not come."

He calls every day. The daily phone calls last only a minute since, as a cash-strapped student, he can only afford to put two German marks on the international calling card, but it is enough for me to just hear him say my name. Oh, how I wish I could see him again.

And yet, because of the four years that I spent every day with my sister Rita, retelling her stories she'd once told to me of her happy childhood in Berlin, my fear of going to Germany is becoming slightly tempered with a kind of curiosity and excitement about the place where my murdered family had once lived.

He's in my dreams at night and in my daydreams during the day. All I think about are his luscious lips and how they would feel on mine. I am filled with lust and longing. I know I'm not being at all rational, that I am not thinking clearly, actually not at all, about my lifelong fear of all things German or about Jannek's age. I tell myself that this plane ticket to Munich that I cannot afford—but which the Delta reservation agent has booked using my frequent flyer miles (from the fundraising trips I took throughout the country on behalf of the UJA)—is another sign from God.

So, four months from the day we first met, I fly to him on the evening of September 10, 2001.

He is waiting at the Munich airport when I arrive the next day. It is a beautiful, sunny afternoon. I am too embarrassed to rush into his waiting arms, so I give him my cheek for a light kiss hello. Because the form is in German, he helps me fill out the lost luggage report for my missing suitcase.

We drive in the mud-caked, dented car he'd borrowed to the apartment of his Czech classmate Ivana, who has agreed to sublet her place to me while she travels through the Middle East. Expecting the apartment to be empty, I am surprised that Ivana is still there and watching television. Feeling somewhat uncomfortable that she is home, and that she has not lifted her eyes to greet me, I just gaze at the screen. It shows a plane flying into the Twin Towers of the World Trade Center in New York, and because I hear a man speaking German, I smile, thinking that this must be a German-dubbed action-packed *Die Hard*-style film, or maybe it's a new Spiderman movie. I am waiting for the hero to appear to stop the plane from hitting the tower when suddenly I hear Jannek scream, "Oh my God! No, no, no!" He rushes to my side and through his choking sobs translates for me the German newscaster who is reporting on a terrorist attack. I am in shock, unable and unwilling to grasp his words.

"I have to go home," I shout to Jannek. All the airports are closed. Ivana's trip to the Middle East has been postponed indefinitely.

Jannek does not return to his dormitory room as we had planned. He will not leave me alone now, so we share Ivana's studio apartment and sleep on twin mattresses on the floor. The television stays on day and night, but Ivana is not a big fan of America or its people, showing little sympathy for what has happened to New York, my home. Jannek and I wait until she falls asleep, and with Enya singing "A Day Without Rain" and the burning towers on the television screen, we just hold each other and weep.

The German newspapers are filled with pictures of the giant towers being hit. Candlelight vigils are everywhere. Hundreds of flowers are lovingly placed on the steps of churches and storefronts with notes, letters, and handmade posters covered with pictures of the once-looming towers. On them the Germans have written, "We are Americans too!"

In silent solidarity they stand in line in the rain with me for hours just to sign the condolence book in the lobby of the US Consulate General. With open hearts they reach out, giving me a hand to hold, a kind word, a sympathetic smile, a bouquet of flowers, a prayer of strength, or just a warm embrace.

But alas, this German lovefest does not last. As soon as it is rumored in October that there will be an American invasion of Afghanistan, the protests begin. I am in Berlin with Jannek, standing among the thousands of people from all over the country who have gathered at the Brandenburg Gate to march. They carry signs of a smiling President Bush with a Hitler mustache and chant, "No more war!" Banners that read "The Ugly American" fly from flowered balconies.

I struggle to stay in the present with the frenzy of the protests and the roar of the men and woman who march, but I keep seeing scenes of an earlier time when the Germans were similarly frenzied, running through the streets at a fevered pitch, shouting, "Death to the Jew!" I want to run away. I am afraid that they will harm me, the mocked American and the once-hated Jew.

This is my America they are reviling. She had opened her arms and heart and welcomed the seven-year-old, lice-covered orphaned refugee who I had been. My loyalty to America is not political, and I will not admit how sad and angry I am at my president, who had spoken so passionately at Ground Zero about the courage and strength and freedoms that we Americans hold so dear, but who has made a terrible, terrible mistake. I want to scream at all these Germans in the street,

"How dare you! Have you forgotten how my Americans flew airlifts of food to the starving German people after the war? Have you forgotten that the Marshall Plan, with its tax dollars from the American people, provided the resources, materials, labor, and money that helped rebuild Germany to make her the powerful, rich country she is today?"

But I say nothing. I am paralyzed with fear.

This demonstration has turned me against all things German now. The outpouring of love and grief, and the posters that read, "We are Americans too," were just a mirage.

"No, Jannek. I will not speak at the university. No way. No Germans for me."

A week later the airports are reopened and Ivana is able to leave. I stay.

Jannek and I are alone and grabbing at each other's clothes. Sixty-two years old, I no longer resemble the Botticelli nude of my youth. Instead I am a nude with varicose veins, flabby thighs, a loose potbelly, saggy breasts, a disappearing waistline, wide hips, and a large cellulite-covered rear, but I still have beautiful hazel eyes and a smile that lights up a room. For just a moment I fear that I might hurt the underdeveloped, thin, inexperienced body of this beautiful twenty-two-year-old boy, on whose penis I sit, but then I remember that he's never been with a woman and my weight won't matter at all.

Nine hours later, with only two half-hour breaks in which he massaged my leg cramps and helped me walk to the bathroom, I ask him where and how he has learned to do what he's just done to me. With that beautiful smile, he shyly confesses that he owes it to the porno films that he and his ninety-year-old Slovakian grandfather have watched every New Year's Eve from the time he was nine while his grandmother slept in the other room.

We spend every possible moment together. One month later, Ivana is home. I rent a studio apartment on the floor below. Every month I pay the rent and our living expenses from my checking account, which has only Social Security deposits as income. With the exchange rate and transfer fees from bank to bank, I no longer have what was once a very healthy US account. Jannek has a part-time job doing research for a professor at the university, which pays for his books and tuition.

With no friends and not speaking the language, I cling to Jannek, afraid to venture out by myself. My self-doubt and insecurity feed into Jannek's need to dominate and control me. Six months later his adoration and undivided attention begin to stifle me.

"What did you and Herr Schmidt talk about? Why did you stand so close to him? Tell me why he was smiling at you," he demands.

I'm not sure what I am supposed to feel; these scenes that play out between us are so bizarre that I don't even know how to stay in the room. I just want to laugh.

We are living in a studio apartment in Munich, and the stress of living in such close quarters with a woman forty years his senior makes him increasingly short-tempered and volatile, until I grow terrified of setting him off. When he is not in school I am home alone with Jannek and I begin to feel trapped. His angry outbursts and his demands that I never go anywhere without him are no longer endearing or a sign of how much he loves me, but rather how emotionally insecure he is. Our quarrels have become tiresome and boring.

In 2002, on a breezy, sun-filled morning with Jannek pouting and sullen yet again, I open my computer and there is a German document in my email. Looking annoyed, Jannek finally consents to translate it for me.

Dear Ms. Gutmann,

We wish to inform you that your request to become a German citizen has been granted. You have strong ties to Germany because of your parents and their fate. You will keep your American citizenship as well. Please be in my office at 2 pm, when you will be sworn in.

Frau Scheffer
Köln, Germany

* * *

"You promised that you would come with me," I plead.

"Go without me!" Jannek shouts.

I am being punished again. All I asked was that he not put on his favorite blue shirt. The collar and cuffs are frayed and ripped.

On a rainy summer morning I go alone to Cologne. I stop to ask a stranger on the street, fumbling through a chopped-up German, *"Bitte zeig mir den weg zum Bahnhof."* Please show me the way to the train station.

"Where are you from?" he answers in perfect German-accented English.

"I am an American, but for the past year I've been living here in Munich."

"Oh, America is a very big country. Too big for me, and anyway Bush is running it," answers the stranger. "Besides, you know the Jews are the only ones with the money. They are the ones that really run the country." His words just hang there.

I know it's crazy and completely unfounded to get myself all worked up about it, but once it's unleashed and given enough time and space, my fear completely overtakes me and I am convinced that this man will surely harm me. I feel the history of hate. My parents, forty members of my family, and the men and women and children who died at the hands of a people who thought the Jews were vermin and parasites. I become very still. I find this moment chilling. I believe that I am in danger. I am silent, and I just walk away.

* * *

I am sixty-three years old when I am awarded German citizenship in a cluttered office of the *Bundesverwaltungsamt* in Cologne on a gray, wet July day in 2002.

I sign the Declaration of Loyalty document. When Jannek translates the page to me later, I learn that I have sworn to declare my loyalty to the free and democratic constitutional order of the Basic Law of the Federal Republic of Germany. In particular, I recognize: the people's right to choose the authority of the state through elections and the right to vote for the representation of the people through direct, free, equal, and secret ballot.

I register with Democrats Abroad and send my absentee ballot to America when I vote for the president in 2004.

How ironic that what I had begun on behalf of my parents in America, my home, is awarded to me in Germany, my parents' home. This light-green German naturalization certificate signed by Kartheiser and stamped with the winged eagle, a kind of German coat of arms, that my gentle, Leipzig-born, Berlin-loving father had not been "pure" enough to have, was only symbolic for me. I never intended to use it. I could never live permanently in Germany. I thought I would put the document away somewhere and probably never look at it again.

* * *

The mind-numbing attraction I've had for Jannek is fading. His mood swings and his childish temper tantrums are exhausting. He is very dysfunctional. He thrives on creating chaos and outrage. I'm even bored with the wild sex that always follows the screaming and crying and ranting.

Early in our relationship Jannek told me how much he had struggled to make it on his own. That he went against the wishes of his possessive mother and left his home in Prague at age seventeen. He was accepted (one of the youngest) at the famous Ludwig-Maximilian University in Munich.

His mother was so angry that he had refused to study medicine and chose political science instead that she sent him to the university holding onto a suitcase made of cardboard. It held two pairs of underpants, a pair of jeans, a blue shirt (the one he wore when we met), and the small, blue blanket he'd used as a child. He laid the blanket on the floor and covered himself with newspapers for several months.

Like an addict I am hooked—caretaking and rescue is my drug. I am completely swept up by my obsession. It's this strange theme that underlies my relationships with men. This compulsive longing, almost like a hunger I have, for love and attention. I even trick myself into believing that the money I am spending on Jannek is an investment. He needs me. I will embrace and support the dream that his mother would not.

I try and persuade him not to go. "Jannek, you're crazy to travel to Slovakia in this weather. You will miss two days of school. You can't afford that. All your mom needs is to hear your voice. Just call her," I beg.

But, on an ice-cold winter morning he travels seventeen hours each way on an old, unheated train, to visit with his beloved "Mamka" in the hospital. He sleeps on the bench outside her room until she wakes up from surgery. He can only stay one hour, but it is enough for her to just see his face.

Their relationship seems Oedipal to me. When he talks to his mother on the phone, although it's in Czech, I can hear by the tone in his voice that it sounds just as flirtatious and intimate as when he and I are in bed. I ask him if she knows about me. I am a secret.

It is so easy to blame Jannek for everything. But, I can no longer deny that it is also my own neurotic need to be needed. I am so busy fixing Jannek that I leave no time for me to think about how frightened and lonely I feel.

I realize that I am jealous too. I act so petty, making fun of his precious Mamka, but I really envy her. I had been such a wise and caring mother, always coming to David's rescue and sparing him any hardships, yet months will pass until I even hear from him.

* * *

Now I will go back to America, my home. But no, I will not. For suddenly I feel something stirring beneath my surface, like a hazy recognition of something new. It is a new awareness. I thought that Jannek was the reason I had come to Germany, when a memory surfaces. I am sitting with my sister Rita in her Cleveland kitchen as she tells me the stories of the parents that I do not remember and of her early, happy life in Berlin. The journey that has brought me here had really begun forty years earlier in that Cleveland kitchen. When Rita died I needed to understand and find my own answers and my own story. So I will begin to look. And, with Rita tucked safely in my heart, I begin a new life.

I am in the Rathaus Schöneberg, a town hall in Berlin, to apply for a German Identification Card. I think it is no accident that the lovely, smiling woman who helps me with the paperwork is a redhead like Rita, like the kind doctor who demanded the removal of Rita's feeding tube, and like my mama. Jannek and Annette, our Berlin friend, are with me to translate, but when the woman asks for information about my parents, Malcha and Nathan Gutmann, I do not wait for the English translation. Instead, "Auschwitz" is all I say.

Filled with sorrow, on the verge of tears, I close my eyes and raise my head toward the ceiling as if it was heaven, and I whisper to my parents, "This German citizenship is for you!"

When I open my eyes, the kind civil servant is crying.

I commit to resurrecting my murdered family and the life they had once lived, and to do that, I realize that I must live in Berlin.

CHAPTER FORTY-ONE

MY OWN BERLIN

One morning I get out of bed, pack a single suitcase, write a short note explaining why I left, get a cab to the main train station, and, while Jannek is visiting his family in Prague, I go to Berlin. I rent an apartment of my own on a quiet tree-lined street a twenty-minute subway ride from Tiergarten, the last neighborhood where my parents and sisters lived before they were forced to flee. "It is my wish that you find peace and happiness in your new home" is written on the rental agreement by the eighty-year-old German landlord with whom I have shared the fate of my parents.

"Go away, Jannek," I shout through the intercom. I imagine how Jannek must have cried and pleaded with Annette to tell him where I lived.

"Please, Schätzelein," he replies with his pet name for me. "Let me in."

But before I can answer, there is a loud knock on my apartment door. I open the door and expect to see the sweet, loving Jannek I'd heard through the intercom. The Jannek who brushes past me and into my living room is belligerent and arrogant. I know this Jannek. He is ready to wage war.

"No, Jannek, you cannot live with me. It's too hard. I am tired of hearing you complain. First it's that I only listen to classical music, or that I get up too early, or that the coffeemaker wakes you, or how you don't understand why you have to wash your smelly feet before you come to bed." I can't say I was miserable every day we lived together in Munich, but I was constantly anxious and self-conscious, never able to fully relax.

I don't tell him that he has become a financial burden, that I am tired of his inappropriate and childish behavior when he screams his silly accusations at me. (They bring back an unwelcome memory of Aunt Gerdy with her doomy voice as she predicted, after that pregnancy when I was seventeen, that she knew that I would never amount to anything.) His back-and-forth manic need to create chaos and drama was making me crazy and angry.

Because Dr. Wainberg helped me find the self-respect that I had lost, now Jannek can no longer fight my need to regain my self-respect. I will never again give up fighting to hold onto my new fought-for autonomy and freedom.

"I am hard to live with, Jannek. I am set in my ways and I won't change. I need my own space."

Because he wants to be close to me and since I do not want him out of my life, just out of my home, Jannek finally agrees to live in the student housing that Humboldt University in Berlin will provide him. He pays for it by working as a waiter in the Wintergarten café on the second floor of the elegant Literaturhaus Berlin, four times a week.

As soon as Jannek tells me that he is having sex with a woman he met at work, and that he does not wear a condom, it is the end of sex for me. Until that point I still had occasional sex with this beautiful, romantic, smiling boy/man. It was always fluid and easy and laced with laughter. Now I am totally turned off. I warn him about having unsafe sex, but he is young and arrogant. "I can't feel anything wearing that thing," he whines.

I pack away my sexy underwear and my come-fuck-me shoes (red satin, high-heeled, and decorated with bright stones on the ankle straps and which I could only wear lying down in bed).

What a subtle, treacherous mistake I made. How dishonest of me to have seen Jannek as anything more than a fling. Just for fun and sex, it could have been fine for me to play a game like that with this beautiful boy. For me to deny and ignore this is just crazy and wrong. But now I know that I was under the sway of my own deflated ego, a complicated form of self-loathing, shame, and codependent craziness. I'd even tricked myself into believing that it was love. I am not proud of my lack of restraint and self-indulgence. What happened to all that self-esteem I'd worked so hard to build?

But now we have something real, like a friendship. He is my personal computer guy, my German translator, and my tour guide. I am his confidante, his English translator, his armchair therapist, and his best friend.

I am sitting with Jannek and Herr Bloch, the director of the *Entschädigungsbehörde* (Office of Reparation), five months after submitting the twenty-page application that Jannek helped me fill out. I am nervous about this meeting, since my caseworker said that her other applicants never do this.

To my surprise, this proper German man has found a loophole and a way to offer me the German pension, which only someone born in Germany receives. "Because your mother was pregnant with you, I believe you would have been born in Germany had your family not been forced to flee," said a smiling Herr Bloch. How moved I am when Jannek translates Herr Bloch's words.

Herr Bloch has made it financially easier for me to stay.

CHAPTER FORTY-TWO

FACING HISTORY

Jannek has a class, so I must find my way alone to Grunewald. I am excited to visit the park where my family had once picnicked on Sundays. I am riding the *S-Bahn*, the aboveground train, and the first thing I see when I depart the train at Grunewald is a memorial plaque on the station wall in memory of the more than fifty thousand Jews who were deported between October 1941 and March 1945 by the National Socialist state. Most of these Jews were transported from the Grunewald train station to the extermination camps.

This is *Gleis 17*, the infamous Track 17. At first the trains left for the ghettos of Lodz and Warsaw, but in 1942 they started going directly to Auschwitz or other concentration camps and death camps. As I walk to the stairs that lead up to the track, I pass a concrete block embedded with human silhouettes. This represents the passage where the Jews were marched onto the loading bay.

I am caught off-guard when I see in the concrete block the silhouette of an old, bent, kerchief-wearing woman holding the hand of a small child. I lose all control and just weep at the sight. As I walk beside a long stretch of the original track, I read all 186 steel-cast plaques set in the ground next to the platform's edge. They are in chronological order, beginning with the first transport and ending with the last transport—of eighteen Jews from Berlin to the Theresienstadt camp on March 27, 1945, *only one month before the end of the war.* It was a German act of *Alles in Ordnung,* everything is in order. Germans love order, and this chills me. A hand grenade has hit me and all logic has blown up in my face.

One month before the war ended. How could these SS officers do this? How could they send men, women, children, old people, newborns, pregnant woman, and invalids to be exterminated? They knew about the death camps and the ghettos and the labor camps where the Jews were starved and worked to death. How could you go home and sit with your families and tell them about your day at work? How could you rush those eighteen Jews onto that train when you knew that the end was near? The Nazis knew that the Allies had already bombed Dresden, only two hours away from Berlin. A rage wells up in me and I begin to cry, "How could you?" I shout until I have no more energy or voice left. A small crowd has gathered and they are looking at me. I look at them with hateful eyes and walk defiantly to the tracks. *You're all to blame for what happened here. You in your beautiful villas with your landscaped gardens looked out of your windows and watched this pathetic march of human cargo. And you said and did nothing.*

Each of the 186 steel-cast plaques also states the number of deportees, the point of departure in Berlin, and the destination. The earliest inscription on the plaques is dated October 1941, the day on which 1,251 people were sent to concentration camps at Auschwitz and Lodz. Without the railway (like the *S-Bahn* that I just rode here)—in particular without the

Deutsche Reichsbahn—the deportation of the European Jews to the extermination camps would not have been possible. The vegetation between the rails at Track 17 has been left to grow, says the sign. The grass is a symbol that no more trains will ever depart from this platform. The transports to death for the Jews were even billed to and paid for by the Jewish community: four *Pfennige* were charged per mile for the adults, and the bargain rate of two *Pfennige* were charged for children above the age of four.

There is no one in this beautiful, upper-class, mansion-filled Grunewald suburb who can tell me where to find the exact spot with the café awning in the background like the one in the black-and-white picture I take out from my bag. Taken by Papa in 1936, it shows Mama sitting on the grass beside a tablecloth spread with food, smiling at her brother Julius, who is tickling my laughing sisters, four-year-old Rita and three-year-old Susi. This is the traditional Sunday picnic in Grunewald. Today I want to recreate this scene. I walk for more than an hour, looking for a red-haired, smiling, pretty woman sitting on the grass with her two young, laughing girls, but I am alone, and the only laughter I hear comes from an outdoor café filled with men drinking beer. I am an archeologist here in Berlin, but instead of bones, I search for the parents I do not remember. And because I know how they died, I try to recreate, scene-by-scene, piece-by-piece, the precious moments of the happy life they had once lived here. But I am grasping at ghosts. My parents still do not come alive for me. It is always hard on me when I dig, because at the end of every excavation there will be grief.

* * *

It is New Year's Eve in Berlin. I hear drunken, loud revelers throwing rocks at the telephone booth that sits on the corner of Gosslerstrasse, the quiet, tree-lined street where I live. I go outside, but when I see the shattered glass and listen to the young laughing crowd, I panic, freeze with fear, and run trembling back to my apartment. It is only when CNN shows the ball at midnight in Times Square bringing in the New Year that I calm down. It is not *Kristallnacht* (the Night of Broken Glass when the Nazi storm troopers broke the store windows of all the Jewish shops and set fire to the synagogues in 1938). These young people are not the SS. This is 2003, I am safe, and I have nothing to fear.

***

Three German policemen and several Israeli security personnel stand guard by the front door of a red brick building. I am here for the Friday evening Sabbath service in the synagogue on Pestalozzistrasse. When I open the door, I must wait until security searches through my handbag, then I am told to walk through the electronic opening as if I were at the airport, where a fourth policeman is waiting to buzz me through the glass door that opens to a large courtyard. There in the rear, surrounded by two small apartment buildings and hidden from the street, stands the synagogue. It was partially destroyed in the horror of *Kristallnacht*, three days before my papa's fortieth birthday and one week before the family fled.

With the funds provided by the German government and private donations from Berlin's former Jewish residents, all of whom live abroad or in Israel, the synagogue where my family once worshipped was restored in 1947. A large gold plaque with the words "Six Million Murdered 1933-1945" hangs above the entrance to the sanctuary where I sit next to Brigitte, a woman whom I guess to be around seventy years old. "I worshipped here as a small girl," she whispers. "But that was before my Catholic father had to hide me and my Jewish mother with his family in the countryside until the war ended." I question her, excited, hoping that she will tell me how the synagogue looked then, but she cannot remember.

It has a high-domed ceiling now and a large chandelier hangs over the men's section in the center of the sanctuary. On the bima, the platform, the American rabbi and the Israeli cantor conduct the German service. Inside the Ark, a wooden enclosure draped in blue velvet, sits the Torah. High above the bima, beneath a large, blue, stained-glass window with a gold Star of David in the center, stands the choir, which sings the ancient Hebrew prayers of this service with voices like those I hear at the opera house.

Tonight Jacob sits directly across from me. He and I are just Friday night friends. He will be making *aliyah*—moving to Israel—next month. I will miss seeing him here. He survived the war sheltered as the Christian nephew of his former Berlin neighbors, he told me. Tonight he has brought his grandson. I cannot take my eyes off this adorable, well-behaved little boy whom I guess to be about three years old, earnestly sliding his small index finger under each word of the prayer book his grandfather reads. It is toward the end of the service when I realize that I have been picturing Papa and myself in this scene. How I envy this little boy. How I long to have had even one moment like his to remember.

One hour later, I have come home to Gosslerstrasse and am searching through my handbag when I discover that I am locked out of my apartment, the keys still lying on the shelf of my bookcase. With a sigh of relief, I see that Frau Humann, my neighbor who has a duplicate set of my keys, has her lights on. We have become good friends, this petite, spirited, charming eighty-year-old German grandmother and I. We spend many hours sitting in her living room and looking through her half dozen picture albums of her grandparents, parents, late husband, children, past and present sons-in-law, grandchildren, and her newest addition, a great-grandchild.

Since I have only one picture to show of the four grandparents I never knew and four pictures of my parents, our time together is spent sharing recipes, deciding where the freshest bread can be bought, and talking about all the art that hangs on my wall. She loves to paint. I have hung her framed, watercolor flowers on my wall. We gossip about the drunken past of the sweet gentleman who lives on the top floor, and the joy that I felt as I watched my son get married in Texas. We keep it simple, light, safe.

Tonight when she opens her door, she comments on how stylish I look. We embrace, she hands me my keys, waits till I open my door, and wishes me a good evening.

What I see is that we are just two women with the same prayer for our children, that they are well and happy and that we did a good job. And yet, I cannot help but wonder if this charming woman, who waters my plants when I'm away, who tells me how blessed and secure she feels to have me living next door, would have helped my family. Would she have saved my life?

* * *

My life is so different here. In many ways I feel oddly safe and much calmer than usual in a country whose language I do not completely understand. Life is more relaxed than in America, and yet I greet every day with caution, excitement, hope, and fear. I feel much closer to my family here, but that only makes me even more homesick—for what or for whom or for where, I really don't know. Exiled, I am always here when I want to be there. I am addicted to a lost past and forever shopping for a home.

But I make a promise to my family. I will make being here count. I will go to a German language class.

* * *

I am meeting Jannek at Berlin's Sony Center and am waiting on the station platform for the train when I see a large bowl filled with water for dogs to drink. These Germans are the same people who thought my parents, German Jews, were less than human, not deserving of the kindness they show their dogs; this cannot find a rational place in my thoughts. I am cowering, trapped in the train with fifty loud, drunken, banner-waving soccer fans singing a German victory song. Quickly my hand touches the gold Star of David that hangs from my neck, and I place it inside my shirt. To me this large, out-of-control crowd has become the Hitler Youth. Their banners display a swastika. The song they sing is *"Deutschland über alles."* "Germany above all else." There is no one to stop the fall. I am hurled into a past that always lies on my skin. The demons come uninvited, without warning, and I am never prepared emotionally for the impact of living with the dead.

* * *

Another time, I am walking into the KaDeWe department store when a well-dressed, charming elderly couple who are walking behind me tap me on the shoulder and politely ask if they can tuck the designer tag on the neck of my shirt back inside. "It's not nice if it shows," says the woman. I smile politely and nod my head. I am reminded of the time I walked out from my New York apartment, to visit Milton's grave, and I wore two different shoes and my shirt was inside out and no one even noticed.

Once again I think back to that time and I think that maybe the Jews just did not fit in. That they were the only ones who believed they were German Jews. Then I realize that they were always *Jews in Germany* and not "pure Germans."

* * *

I have been searching unsuccessfully in all the bakeshops in Berlin for the sugar-glazed, slivered almond-topped, cream-filled torte called *Bienenstich,* just like the one that came from the German bakery on the corner of 160th Street, a block from where I lived with my Daddy Sam, Aunt Gerdy, and Michel and Stuart. I can still smell this torte more than forty years later. The search resurrects other memories of my immigrant neighborhood in New York. There was also Orner's German Restaurant, four blocks away, where every Sunday evening we met other refugee friends, after the soccer game in which my new daddy had played. I always ate the pot roast with potato pancakes and spoonfuls of the free cucumber salads, coleslaw, and German potato salads on the table. But it was the German deli two blocks up from Orner's where there was *cevelat*—a pork-and-beef, artery-clogging German salami that

I ate sliced extra-thick, between two even thicker slices of fresh mayonnaise-covered pumpernickel bread—the memory of which still makes my mouth water.

All the wonderful places of my youth that had been opened by German Jews—I think I am looking for them. How tragic it was that they had been forced to leave. And I think about what Germany has lost as a result. By ridding herself of her Jews, she has lost a piece of her diverse history and soul.

* * *

I have just exited the subway at Walther-Schreiber-Platz and am walking to the Karstadt department store when I see a large double-sided sign, what we in the States call a sandwich board. It sits on the sidewalk in front of a jewelry store. *"Wir kaufen Zahngold und Altgold,"* reads the sign. "We buy dental gold and antique gold." I stand with my mouth open, unable to breathe, and I wonder if maybe not all the gold from my parents' teeth had been melted, and maybe some old Nazi might have some lying in a drawer that he will sell someday.

This is not the Germany of Washington Heights where I grew up among German-Jewish Holocaust survivors, who refused to speak their mother tongue, and who never talked, not even to each other, about the treasured home they had been forced to leave. Berlin is a haunted city, covered in memorials to the murdered Jews, but among the ten thousand Jewish people who live here—young Israelis and Russians, who have a very weak Jewish identity, thanks to the Soviet era—there are almost no German-born Jews who survived the Holocaust and remained in Berlin. For me, it is a city where I often walk through emotional minefields.

But just as the Germans are a constant reminder to me of what their grandparents did, I am also a constant reminder to them. Maybe this is why I am here. Maybe it is so we can finally look at each other with different eyes. Our legacy connects us. Our wounds make us more the same than different.

CHAPTER FORTY-THREE

A NEW WORLD OF LOVE

Because I had not spoken at the University of Munich in 2001, and because I had promised to make being in Berlin count, I ask Jannek to transcribe a letter in 2004. It says that I am a hidden child survivor of the Holocaust, an American living in Berlin, the once cherished home of my parents, and that I wished to share my story of survival with German students as I have often done at schools in America. Would the directors be interested in me sharing the story of my family's fate and its shattered aftermath? The letter also states that I am requesting the school to pay me an honorarium of 100 Euro and that the students must understand English. We send it to the directors of all twenty *Gymnasien,* German high schools that we find listed in the 2003 phone book.

I am conflicted and I sway between hoping that the schools do not respond and hoping that they will. Although I was really scared when Jannek's German professor in Auschwitz pleaded with me to share my story of survival with his German group, I felt much safer and more protected because of the American students in the room that night.

The first invitation to come and speak comes from the Leonardo-da-Vinci Gymnasium. The letter, written in English, promises that all the seventeen-year-old high school history students understand English much better than they speak it.

I am told to be there at 7:45 in the morning and that the history teacher will meet me at the entrance and bring me to the room where I will speak. It will be a large group, since there are so few survivors in Berlin who wish to speak, and never one from America; they have invited an English class and two more afternoon history classes will attend. There will be a hundred students in the room.

It is still dark when I arrive. I am wrapped in a foggy, cold November morning. A smiling Frau Schultz welcomes me. "Come, the students are waiting for you." As I had requested of the school director, a hundred desks and foldout chairs are arranged in a circle where the students sit. There are not enough chairs so students are sitting on tables in the back of the room and cross-legged on the floor. I stand before the teacher's desk in the front of the room with the students surrounding me.

I immediately pick up the energy; it feels like I have walked into a room full of explosives and I am the lit cigarette. My heart is racing. I feel nauseous and dizzy and my head is throbbing. I sense that this hour will be counted and graded and that it is the only reason the students are here. The students are yawning and bored, and look at me with eyes that say nothing.

"Someone help me!" I want to scream, but the words are trapped in my throat. I want to run out of this claustrophobic room, but I cannot move. I muster up all my faith and strength to get calm and still when I begin to feel that we are not alone in the room—and that the spirits of my parents and all those who were slaughtered are here to protect me. *Tell them who we were,* they plead.

"Good morning. Thank you for coming," I tell this seemingly inhospitable and arrogant group of teenagers as I walk around the circle and shake their hands, hoping to ease the sense of apprehension that I pick up in the room. And the room shifts. The air is relaxed and light. After this very solemn start, my story begins to unfold.

"When I called my eighty-five-year-old friend Ava in America to tell her that I would be speaking with you today, she spat out, 'Kill them all!' She had not a trace of the charming Hungarian accent I am used to hearing from this Holocaust survivor, who had survived four German labor camps and Auschwitz. It is not the voice that sounds just like the pecan-filled cookies she bakes and sends me.

"Upon my arrival at age seven in America, I had lost my parents, my grandparents, aunts, uncles, young cousins—forty in all. I'd even lost my birth name Ruth, which was dangerously too Jewish. Hitler had stolen my language, my home, my childhood, and my memory.

"Ignorance creates genocide and war. It is indifference that was the cause of genocide then, and now."

I show the students my pain and anger when I say, "How enthusiastic the German people were about Hitler. Get rid of those parasites and vermin and leeches!"

I hold up the sepia-colored photograph of my parents taken in 1930, with Mama looking like a silent film star—curly-haired, wearing a white dress and a rhinestone-encrusted black band around her neck, her hand resting on her hip—and

Papa, her leading man, bow-tied and tuxedoed, a white hankie tucked into his pocket.

"Vermin and parasites. This is what they called my beautiful young mother and my gentle, opera-loving father!" I am unable to back off from saying this with sarcasm and scorn and sorrow.

I do not hold back my tears when I tell them about Rivesaltes, the French internment camp. "The floor of the children's barrack was covered with lice-filled straw. That's where we slept. All we were given to eat were half-filled bowls of rotten tomato soup once a day." I tell them about the latrine outside, with no partitions, just a long, wooden plank with holes to squat over. "It was a long walk alone in the mud for the three-year-old I was then. My ten-year-old sister Rita looked after me because we were only allowed a visit with Mama for two hours a day."

I share with them the day my beautiful red-haired mother was deported. And that her last words before the French police pushed her onto the waiting cattle car were a promise to return. I am engulfed in so much sorrow that I can barely whisper. "The French guards would not let my brave mother hold me, or whisper words of comfort or give me a kiss good-bye, before she left me and my two sisters in the care of the stranger who would save our lives."

I feel my throat tighten and I want to hide the tears welling up inside of me. "To lose your mother is to lose your anchor to the world. A mother is the all-nurturing center of the universe to a little girl—the woman who should have lived and formed the essence of the woman I would become. The damage that is done to children in wars and other traumatic situations is especially cruel because it lasts for life."

The room is still. No one yawns or coughs or clears their throat. They don't move or shift uncomfortably in their seats. They sit like statues with every eye fixed on me. I can hear the pounding of hearts, mine included. As I look around the room I see shiny, wet eyes. The girls are crying openly. The boys sniffle and look away.

These teenagers have taken me in. Their hearts are open. They will journey with me through the sorrow, the guilt, the anger, and the love. It is not so long ago that they were three years old, or maybe they have a brother or sister who is three now. They can relate to the unimaginable pain that Mama and her children suffered that day. Who will love me? Who will sit on my bed and read to me until I fall asleep? Who will cook for me? Who will take care of me when I'm sick? This is what they worry about now. I can see it on their faces. I hear it in their sobs. Afraid and lost like I had been then.

"It has been so hard for me to reconcile that the way my parents showed me their love was very different than the way your parents and parents everywhere show their love. My mother did not take me to Auschwitz and my father had Mademoiselle Rothschild, a member of the clandestine organization saving Jewish children, promise to smuggle us to safety in Switzerland. Then he was arrested and murdered in the camp.

"Hitler meant for me to die. My parents meant for me to live. And I save my parents' lives each time I speak.

"Of course I'm damaged. How does it fit in any normal logic that when I think of my parents I pray to God that they went straight to the gas chamber? How can that be normal?"

I have conjured up the Nazi death machine and placed it in this room for these young German students. I feel the tight grip the death machine has on me. But there is no escape—and really no time has passed at all since my parents were shoved into a cattle car marked with a sign that read "Suitable for eight horses" and crammed in with a hundred men and women, boys and girls, the heavy sliding doors tightly locked and entwined with barbed wire, the outside world only visible to the human cargo through narrow, slatted openings originally designed to provide just enough air to keep the cattle alive for the slaughterhouses of Europe.

"There is power in naming hate for what it is, in shining a bright light on it, brighter than a torch or a flashlight. When we name it, we root it out of the darkness, out of all that hushed conversation where it breeds like vermin. We must acknowledge and confront it. When we do that, we rob it of its power and its dark pull.

"The guilt and shame that has silenced you, but that really belonged to your ancestors, was the beast that hovered in the room. And only when we look at it, as you and I have done today, can we begin the healing. Yours and mine!

"Because I am wounded myself, I have a very good sense of the wounds in you. I know what a frail business life is. And since there are so few survivors in Germany to bear witness, here is where I feel the most needed.

"Never let anyone rob you of your voice. All you can do against injustice and hate is to open your mouths and speak. Don't look away. Make a difference. Tell someone you love him or her every day!

"My hope for a more peaceful future rests on your shoulders, even though I know how difficult that burden will sometimes feel. Remember that life is a gift every day—even broken, imperfect and poorly wrapped—but a gift nevertheless."

I write my name and my email address on the blackboard behind me. "Please send me your thoughts, and your hopes, and your fears. Do not be afraid. I will never share what you write me with anyone. Write me in German if that is easier for you."

The silence in the room frightens me; I am certain that they are angry with me. But then I hear a hundred chairs sliding back, bodies rising. Chanting, "We love you!" the students stand and give me five minutes of nonstop thunderous applause. I break down in tears. I can't get out another word. I am mortified by my public display. Germans don't generally do that. They hold back. But they rush into my open arms, wanting only to touch my cheek with their own wet cheeks, to stroke my hair, to hold my hand just to say, "Thank you."

"We will never forget you. We will remember your family. We will make a difference. We will put more love in the world."

I linger for another hour as people line up to tell me their stories. One girl has three small silver hoops hanging from her nose, tiny metal buttons on her lip and tongue, two tiny hoops in her eyebrow, and a bright purple streak in her hair on the side that is not shaved. From the corner of my eye, I try reading her blank face. Afraid of what someone so outwardly a model of protest and aggression will say or do, I greet her with a frozen smile. But she pulls me into her arms and whispers; "You have changed my life today. Tell your friend in America that we are not like that, and that if she comes here we will show her who we are. You made us feel proud to be Germans today!"

I gather up the beautiful bouquet of flowers the class has given me, and the three laminated photographs of Mama, Papa, and me, and just as I am about to leave the room, I feel a hand on my shoulder. I turn around and see that it is Frau Schultz, the students' history teacher. She had quietly left the room ten minutes before I finished my talk.

"Frau Gutmann, my father was a proud member of the Gestapo in charge of rounding up the Jews. I have kept that secret for fifty years."

I am trapped. No, no, I don't want to hear this. This is too in my face, too personal. I feel the fear and anger welling up inside of me, but I cannot walk away. I am forced to let her continue.

"Since I am also a mother, I could relate to the suffering of parents who were forced to leave their children behind when they discovered that they themselves would be deported. Your story tore my heart apart. It is so important that you have chosen to tell your story, since we likely won't have the opportunity to hear the witnesses for much longer. I am so grateful that a Jewish woman who has lost everything has come to Germany to speak of peace."

CHAPTER FORTY-FOUR

OUT OF HIDING

I am filled with strange new feelings. Were these young, shame-filled, guilt-stricken students the Germans I have feared? Are they the monsters I had learned to tame? Can they be related to the goose-stepping, shiny black-booted, and *Heil Hitler-*saluting murderers of my parents and the forty members of a family I never knew? Can they still be the ones who always force me to touch my pain and my tragic loss? Something has changed. I am in new territory, yet I am not afraid. These students have nudged me away from my self-righteous and smug assumptions. I gave them what I most need myself: love.

Perhaps my love is no more than a leap of faith, yet it is one that I nevertheless embrace. This one is a very different love affair than the one I once had with Jannek. This love affair I repeat, once or twice a week as I speak to Christian groups, at universities, at a summer retreat for the grandchildren of both the perpetrators and Holocaust survivors, and to senior citizen groups, acting as a catalyst for open, honest sharing of the past.

* * *

When I read their letters, their emails, and their essays, tears wet my eyes. I am good for my promise; I am making my time in Berlin count.

Sylvia Gutmann came to our school today to speak to us about her experience during the Holocaust. We were told as much in advance, but after her talk we understood that this visit was much more than that. Sylvia and her sisters survived only because some individuals overcame their fear and powerlessness and rescued innocent children.

This woman came to us and told us her story, but she did not tell it the way such stories are read in books or seen in films, but rather, she spoke her story directly to our hearts. Although we have studied the Nazi period, and know the facts and have visited the death camps, where we had frequently been moved to tears, the words of this woman were more meaningful than any book, film, or memorial.

She spoke of her hatred for the German people and how a culture that had produced an Einstein, a Freud, Schiller, and Beethoven could have made it possible for Hitler to rise to power. But she also told us of her return to Germany and how the guilt and shame she saw in the generations so far removed from the Hitler time has changed her.

She asked what each of us would do to spread tolerance, love, and freedom throughout the world, even if it is only in our own small personal environment. Many people say that what happened then could never happen again, but it is apparent that it happens daily around the world. People kill each other over their beliefs and power and money, she says. Neo-Nazis abound, spreading their hate.

Sylvia asked me what I would do. I answered that I would make it my job to spread truth in the world.

* * *

Dear Sylvia Ruth,

My name is Miriam. Your life is so amazing and you grabbed our attention. I think what you do in teaching young people like me about the worst experience in our history, and what we must learn from it, is a blessing. You are a very powerful speaker. Your story is serious, intense, emotional, educational and scary.

Your talk helped me grow. I don't think I will ever look at the world the same way I did before you came to speak. I can promise you that I will take much less for granted and I will make my life more positive.

* * *

Dear Sylvia Ruth,

When we went to the Jewish Museum in September, the tour was very informative; it was nice to see the tour guide so passionate about what he was showing our nursing school class.

At the end of the tour was the talk by the contemporary witness, Sylvia Gutmann. I was expecting an old individual, probably someone difficult to understand, who recalled the past vaguely. Thus, I sat down, took out my pen and my notepad, ready to write down important events. Ms. Gutmann began by introducing herself and I scribbled down: birth date, siblings, etc. It occurred to me that she was not actually that old and that everything she experienced was not so long ago. I put my notepad away.

Ms. Gutmann's warmth and sincerity was so unbelievably empathetic that she allowed me to take her in. Not only because she survived everything but also because she managed to keep her soul intact. Her heart was so big that she could also take us in. I am a better human, nurse, mother, and wife because I heard her talk to us today.

* * *

The radio interviews and the local newspapers that have been covering my talks all speak of my message of love, hope, and forgiveness. They write that I spread seeds of hope, that I build a bridge of understanding, and that compassion is what I preach.

I have a new circle of friends and colleagues who are also my peers. I see how much I have missed being with people who have had life experiences that can only come with age. I tell Jannek he needs to be with people his own age. I sense that secretly he looks relieved when I say that one day he will find a woman with whom he can plan a future, a family. "I want to meet your children someday, but you better not wait too long. I don't want to meet them from a wheelchair," I say with a chuckle.

We cling together when I whisper, "Thank you for being my entry to a place that is haunted by the ghosts of my past. Without you I would never have had the courage to come here."

CHAPTER FORTY-FIVE

MY FATHER'S VOICE

On a snow-covered night in December 2003, I attend a performance of Mozart's *The Magic Flute* at the beautiful *Berlin Staatsoper* (Berlin State Opera), located on the main boulevard, *Unter den Linden*, in what used to be the center of East Berlin. It has crystal chandeliers, thick wine-colored carpet, and plush red velvet seats. I call it "Papa's House."

The sepia-colored photograph that I keep on my desk like a shrine shows my papa and a friend walking down a Berlin street. Papa is wearing a dark jacket, light slacks, a bow tie, and a white shirt. His wide-brimmed hat is worn slightly tipped to the left, a white handkerchief is neatly tucked in his jacket pocket, and his raincoat hangs on his arm. His equally dapper-looking friend carries a cane.

I see him with his dark, fine hair combed straight back, high forehead on a narrow face, and his barely curved, stooped frame; he's a season ticket holder of a balcony seat.

It is here in this very same opera house that a dramatic family story took place, the one that Papa's sister, Aunt Edith, told my sister Rita in Cleveland, Ohio, forty years after this photo was taken. Hermann Göring, the commander-in-chief of the *Luftwaffe* (the German air force) who was later named

Reichsmarschall and designated successor to Hitler, was at the opera house the same evening in 1934 when Papa was there. During the intermission, as Göring stood in the lobby with his comrades, laughing and making fun of all "these Jews," he noticed my elegant father standing across from him. Göring turned to him, bowed his head slightly, and said, "Of course, sir, we have no problem with a Jew like you." I never asked my sister how Göring knew that Papa was a Jew, but when I look at that sepia-colored photograph I have on my desk, I realize that Papa's dark hair and long nose, which the Nazi propaganda machine reported were the features belonging to the "Jew," gave him away.

I am unprepared for the flood of sensations I feel as I wander back to a moment in 1958, when I was a nineteen-year-old hairdresser working in an exclusive salon on New York's Madison Avenue. I had never heard a piece of classical music. As a Christmas gift, my client Mrs. Miller, one of the largest benefactors of the Metropolitan Opera, gave me her front-row seat at the old Metropolitan Opera house on 34th Street and Broadway for the opening night performance of *La Bohème*. The great Renata Tebaldi was singing the role of Mimi.

When I entered that great hall, I was a fat, lonely, and self-loathing high school dropout, an orphaned refugee living with my murdered mother's brother, his wife, and their two sons in Washington Heights.

The old Met was only a hundred blocks away from my neighborhood, but when I heard Mimi, Rodolfo, Marcello, and Musetta sing of their friendship, rapture, passion, and undying love, this was the world that I secretly harbored in my imagination. Washington Heights felt as if it could have been another country.

But now as I sit in the beautiful *Staatsoper* in Berlin, I feel a yearning ache—I am drenched in longing and grief for all the moments, hours, days, and years that I was not allowed to have with my papa. And yet, the tears that sting my eyes are also tears of gratitude for how he had the foresight and courage to save us. Papa was penniless, alone in hiding, so gravely ill that when Mademoiselle Rothschild brought his three daughters back to him after Mama was deported, he could not keep us. Sensing his own imminent arrest in 1943 by the Vichy police, my brave father made contact with Mademoiselle again, pleading to have his three beloved daughters smuggled into Switzerland.

I have no real memory of my parents, of how they looked, how they felt when they held me, or how my mama sounded when she sang me a lullaby. I don't remember how I giggled when Papa kissed me between the rolls of fat on my chubby thighs, or how brave my parents were to pretend to their three young daughters that life was normal in Vichy France in 1942. I realize now that my parents were heroes and that I come from fine stock.

As Mozart's music floats in the air and the story of the opera unfolds, with its dark night, its illuminating path, and its trials and victories, I hear within this magic circle of music a voice from the past that echoes in this great hall. A memory sweeps over me—of my sister Rita and me in her Cleveland kitchen as she shares for the hundredth time her favorite childhood story. It is clear that of all the memories that Rita shares with me, this one is among the most painful, and it always reaches in and grabs me.

"I am six years old," she'd begin. "Mama has dressed me in my yellow-and-white dress. Papa loves this dress most of all, and I only wear it when Papa takes me to the opera house. I love to go with Papa because I am his special little grown-up girl." Rita's voice would often become childlike when she shared this story. But it also made her cry, so she never got to the end of the story and we never left the opera house.

* * *

By 1933, Hitler and the Nazi Party's anti-Semitic rhetoric was gaining strength. The restaurants throughout Berlin displayed signs forbidding Jews from entering. Jews were banned from public transportation and public parks. Jewish teachers, civil servants, journalists, bakers, pharmacists, artists, actors, and musicians were dismissed. The Nazi propaganda also discouraged the German people from visiting Jewish-owned businesses and Jewish doctors and lawyers.

Then came the 1935 Nuremberg Laws. Jews could not own a radio or any electrical device like a phonograph. Jews could not use a public telephone. Jews in Berlin were only allowed to buy food between four and five o'clock in the afternoon (when the shelves were almost empty). Jews were not allowed to own pets. Jewish veterinarians were forbidden to practice. Jews were not allowed to buy sweets.

Every law and every new restriction that the Nazis passed was meant to exclude the Jews from daily life and social structure, and, most of all, to threaten them. These laws shouted, "Parasites! Subhuman! Vermin! Despicable Jews!"

On the evening of November 6, 1938, three days before *Kristallnacht* and four days before my family fled, my papa sat in his beloved Berlin opera house. Despite everything they had taken, the Nazis could not take his soul or the beautiful melodies that stirred the music and the strings of my papa's life.

And on this evening in 2003, I proudly take my place as Nathan's daughter. The joy, the beauty, the thrill, and the rapture that fills me as Sarastro sings to me—this I have inherited from him. Here in this house of magic, of wonder and awe, is where I see my papa with the eyes of my soul. I wave to the balcony from my seat. "I am here, Papa. I am here."

I am here with Sarastro's words reverberating in my heart. *"In diesen heil'gen Hallen Kennt man die Rache nicht."* In this sacred hall, there is no room for revenge. I wrap my beautiful sister Rita and my elegant, gentle papa in my arms as we leave the Berlin opera house together.

CHAPTER FORTY-SIX

SEALED IN STONE

It is an early spring morning in 2004 when I stand in front of the house on Raumerstrasse 21, in Prenzlauer Berg, the former East Berlin. Here sits the apartment building where Mama, Papa, and their two baby daughters lived. Determined to get inside, I ring all the buttons by the door until someone buzzes me in. The lobby sign lists the caretaker's apartment on the second floor. I now knock on his door, grateful to find him home.

"My family once lived here," I rush to tell him, piecing together the words I have learned in the German language course I take at the local high school. I ask, "Is this still the original house?"

"Yes, yes, it was not damaged by the bombs," he assures me.

Everything is still—my breath, my body, and my voice. Frozen, my mind is stunned into silence at his words, surprised and shocked to have heard them. I know it is 2004, yet it feels like I am on a movie set in 1933, waiting for the actors—no, I am waiting for a red-haired, green-eyed, twenty-two-year-old beauty, and an elegantly dressed, slightly stooped-shouldered, opera-loving, twenty-eight-year-old man who sells hair brushes and face creams. I wait for them to come rushing into my waiting arms. *The parents I do not remember but cannot forget!*

This is real! This building, exactly as it was in 1930, when my parents came to start their married life together. There on the landing is the same red, green, and blue-flowered stained glass window next to the winding marble staircase that Mama would have walked down in 1932. She would have been carrying her firstborn, my sister Rita, to a baby carriage, much like the one that is chained to the lobby railing now. Even the fat cherubs carved on the ceiling above the lime green wall tiles might have been there then.

Of all the childhood stories that my late sister so vividly told me, the scene I picture now is Mama getting ready for the Sabbath. She wakes very early on Fridays; there is much to do before sundown. The good dishes are washed, the floors are swept and polished, the furniture is dusted and waxed, and the white linen tablecloth is washed and ironed. Meanwhile, the braided dough for the challah is baking in the oven and the big cast-iron soup pot filled with water, onions, carrots, and the chicken Mama had the butcher slaughter is slowly boiling on the stove.

Only the silver Sabbath candlestick holder is still left for Mama to polish. This is the candelabrum that was returned to Rita in 1974 by a distant cousin who had promised to keep it when my family was forced to flee. Rita left it to her daughter after her death in 1993.

It stands on the special lace cloth that grandmother Rifka crocheted, on top of the dark wood sideboard. Mama will light the candles tonight when she recites the prayer thanking God for the Sabbath.

And, like her blond-haired younger sister Susi, five-year-old Rita with her dark curls has been bathed. Both girls have had their hair washed, combed, and topped off with big white bows. They are dressed in matching pink-and-white pleated cotton dresses, looking like the little dolls of all those childhood stories, waiting for their beloved papa to come home.

The small black suitcase, which Papa carries all week through the neighboring towns and cities to sell his hairbrushes and cosmetics, sits outside the open door where he has dropped it. Calling out for his *"zwei kleine Puppen,"* his two little dolls, he covers the girls with kisses when they run giggling into his open arms.

I picture my grandparents, who come with pockets of candy from the nearby candy store that Papa's mother Chawa owns. I imagine all the aunts, uncles, and young cousins, who came to this house to celebrate the holidays, birthdays, and wedding anniversaries, or just to be together. I want to rewind to that time.

The only part of my parents' life story I know for certain is the tragic end. When I stand in the house where my family once lived, I try to understand what it must have meant for them to have to leave. I want the marble staircase where I now stand, touching the paint-chipped banister that they had once held onto, to finally give me a beginning. Yet all I feel is a deep rage.

I hear the caretaker tell me that he needs to get back to his grandchildren as he waves me good-bye, but his voice sounds far away, like I am in a tunnel, and before I can thank him he's shut the door. There are only two apartments on each floor of this five-story building, and as I turn to leave, I notice the name of the tenant on the apartment door. It sits above a brass slot marked *Briefe*, where the postman drops the mail, and I wonder which apartment once had the name of my family on the door.

There's a young couple on the second floor gardening on their large balcony. They wave to me as I linger on the sidewalk for a last look at the building. I give them a big smile. Oblivious to the people passing by, I shout up to them in English, "My parents Mali and Nathan once lived here!"

Standing in front of this freshly painted light-green house, which for me is the most beautiful one on the street, I tell them about Mama and Papa and my two sisters who were born in the Jewish hospital and then came to this house.

"In which apartment did they live?" they reply in perfect English.

"I do not know. Maybe yours." I smile. I walk slowly back to the *S-Bahn* station, hoping to find a store that looks old enough to have been here when my family lived here. But everything is new in this revitalized, vibrant area of galleries that artists and writers now call home, with new-age crystal shops, organic food stores, and open, loft-like apartments. I could be walking on the familiar streets of New York's Tribeca or Soho.

I stop at a small outdoor café to drink a cappuccino, and I try to imagine the shape my life would have taken if my parents, in fact my very childhood, had not been yanked away from me. I think about all that I have lost. I walk slowly back to the house and write down the name and telephone number of the building's owner that is listed on a small plaque that sits next to the mailboxes.

I make a phone call to the owner. "Hello, Mr. Heilman. I have just come home from Raumerstrasse 21, this house that belongs to you.

"My parents and two older sisters lived in this house, but a week after the November 1938 pogrom, my family fled to

Belgium, where I was born six months later. I am an American, but now I live in Berlin. Throughout Berlin's tree-lined neighborhoods, I have seen plaques that commemorate the murdered Jews, hanging on the outside of the house where they once lived. It is my deepest wish, Herr Heilman, that I too may hang a plaque for my parents who also perished in the camps."

Before I can tell him how happy my family was living in this house, I hear a loud, *"Nein!"* No.

His angry "no" leaves me speechless. "I am only fifty years old," he says. "After the Wall came down in 1989, I had the money to buy and renovate many of the original, architecturally beautiful buildings here in Prenzlauer Berg. I was not born when *that* happened to your family. I take no responsibility. I had nothing to do with it and I don't want any trouble. The local gangs and skinheads have scrawled black Swastikas on other buildings on this block and many other blocks in every neighborhood of Berlin. I do not wish to have this scrawled across the front of my building. If I did this for you, Frau Gutmann, I would have to hang at least three or four plaques for the lost Jews on each of the many buildings I own." He bangs the receiver down.

Well, Mr. Heilman, we'll just see about that, I vow. Is God speaking to me? Is my time in Germany meant to make me more aware of how to be a Jew? Now that I know how to walk the minefields and not get blown up, and because living openly as a Jew in Germany is harder and not always safe because we are a small group here, not like in New York or Miami where there are huge Jewish populations, I will find a way to honor my parents. I am determined to turn his ugly *"Nein!"* into a yes!

* * *

Several months later on my morning walk, I notice a small poster taped to the trunk of a tree. It says that there will be a wine and cheese tasting tonight in the new liquor store that has just opened a few blocks away from where I live. All are welcome. It is not a big space and quite crowded, and because it is a beautiful spring evening, we spill out onto the sidewalk. Here is where I meet Karola, a charming retired civil servant who speaks perfect English. She is warm and bright and I like her right away. It is easy to talk to her, so after I tell her all about my family, and my visit to the house where they had lived, I tell her about Herr Heilman.

"Sylvia, some months ago I read an article about a woman in Freiburg. I believe her name was Marlis. I don't remember where I read the article, but it could only have been in one of the three newspapers my husband Alfred and I have delivered to our door. I remember how touched I was when I read that without the support of the townspeople or Marlis' closest friends, or even the mayor, she wouldn't have found Gunter Demnig, an artist in Cologne whose stumbling stone project Marlis wished to copy. The residents of this lovely, scenic village not far from the Swiss border would have much preferred to keep silent about the Nazi deportations of Freiburg's Jews. I will ask Alfred to look on the Internet for this article. I will call you, Sylvie [I love that she calls me this], as soon as I have some news."

Five months later I sit in the beautifully decorated, book-lined, art-filled apartment of Marlis and her husband Andreas in Freiburg. Tall, big-boned, wide-hipped, large-bosomed, with short, spiked black hair, Marlis resembles a classy, expensively dressed, coquettish, sixty-two year-old hippie. She wears a ring on every finger, and ropes of colored stones hang from her neck. When she laughs it is deep and sexy.

I tell her about my family, about me, and about the upsetting phone conversation I had with Herr Heilman.

"The Nazis ordered the deportation of all of Baden's Jews in 1940," Marlis begins. "Three hundred and fifty Jewish citizens of Freiburg were deported to the southern French internment Camp Gurs in the Basses-Pyrénées region. I searched for a long time to try and find a way to honor and memorialize those forgotten Freiburg Jews. I found the artist Gunter Demnig two years later, but it took another year for me to finally convince him that my commitment to honor Freiburg's once thriving Jewish community was deep. He is not an easy man," warns Marlis.

"What did Gunter do for you?" I ask Marlis.

"Come, let us take a walk," she says in Dinglish, a mix of *Deutsch* and English.

When we walk the cobblestone streets of Freiburg, Marlis stops in front of a beautiful old house and points to a cobblestone cube covered with an inscribed shiny brass plate embedded in the ground. Except for the word *"verhaftet,"* which Marlis must translate for me, I am able to read the German words that are engraved on the brass plate.

Hier wohnte
Karl Balzer
JG. 1885
Verhaftet 1943
Tot 18.12.1943

Here lived
Karl Balzar
Born 1885
Arrested 1943
Died December 18, 1943

"For many years my husband Andreas was my only source of emotional and financial support. Not even my closest friends were happy with my new project and me. Everyone in this *gemütlich*, liberal-minded village would have much preferred to let the Shoah stay safely hidden away and not talked about."

When I hear Marlis, an atheist by choice, a Christian by birth, refer to the Holocaust by its Hebrew name, I am so touched that I pull her into my arms.

Marlis was the first to have reached out to Gunter. She did all the research and found old telephone books and building permits that were submitted in 1940. "Fortunately the bombs that were mistakenly dropped by the German *Luftwaffe* on Freiburg only hit the rail station and not the village. The brass plates that Gunter engraved and laid in the ground in front of the original houses of Freiburg's murdered Jews are called *Stolpersteine*."

* * *

Karola and I are on the bus to Stauffenbergstrasse, where we enter a large courtyard surrounded by a complex of office buildings. This is the Memorial to the German Resistance. It is here where Colonel Claus von Stauffenberg and other members of the failed plot to assassinate Adolf Hitler were executed. I ask Karola to please translate the plaque I see embedded in the ground near the statue of a naked von Stauffenberg.

"You did not bear the shame. You resisted. You bestowed the eternally vigilant symbol of change, by sacrificing your lives for freedom, justice and honor."

I am deeply moved by these words. That a German stood up to his own murderous regime, and held on to his humanity and died for that belief, brings me to tears.

We enter a small, cluttered office of the Stolperstein Initiative Berlin, where a short, gray-haired, elegantly dressed Frau Frankenstein greets me. Wearing a wide smile, she says, "Unless your parents had been Albert Einstein and his wife, of course the owner refused to have your commemorative plaque hung on his private home wall." Frau Frankenstein, the project manager of the Stolperstein Initiative, cannot know how surreal it is when she hands me a 1930 Berlin telephone book. Only heads of the household are listed. I see Raumerstrasse 21, Gutmann, Nathan. His profession is listed as *Kaufmann*, salesman. Wearing a cat-that-ate-the-mouse grin, Frau Frankenstein says, "Sylvia, Herr Heilman does not own the sidewalk. That is public property. It belongs to the city, and we do not need his permission to lay your stones."

* * *

It's a raw December morning in 2005, one year after I made that heartbreaking call to the owner of this building where I now stand. I am holding the laminated sepia-colored photograph of my parents' wedding day as I stand in front of the dark-brown wooden door of Raumerstrasse 21.

Mingling with the huge crowd of people, and speaking German, the language she has not uttered in over sixty years, is my blond-haired, suntanned, seventy-two-year-old sister Susi, who's flown in from Miami for this momentous occasion. Susi had vowed never to come back to Germany, but here she is with her son and her grandson today. We have not spoken since 2001 after I said I was going to Germany. "You're crazy. How can you do this? They are all Nazis!" were the ugly, pointed words she'd hurled at me. After months of struggling to find the courage and the words, I had finally called and asked her to come. And, today her voice is rinsed of that early rage, the tart tongue is in retreat. Our old hurts have vanished when she tenderly embraces me. "I am so proud of you, Sylvia. Thank you for what you did for my parents—*our* parents."

Surrounding me are the many English-speaking high school and university students with whom I have shared the story of my parents' fate. Herr Pentzliehn, the director of the Gustav-Heineman school, and my neighbor Frau Humann are here too. Karola stands next to me, and I notice Frau Frankenstein over on the side. My angels! The kind caretaker Herr Wassner and his charming wife are here as well. And here is the warm embrace of Angelika, my favorite high school history teacher and friend.

Ordained in 2002, Avital Gersteer is the first female Jewish-German cantor in Berlin. Avital sings in the *Neue Synagogue*, the New Synagogue, on Oranienburgerstrasse, and is the first woman after the Holocaust to be allowed to lead a service.

Today these large crowds of people standing on Raumer-strasse 21 listen in awe as the beautiful, curly red-haired, pregnant Avital sings the "Mourners' Kaddish." What I love about this haunting prayer is that it does not mention death or dying or grief; rather it is an affirmation of the holiness of God and the wonder of *life*.

Smatterings of politicians look on; curious pedestrians stop to watch this touching ceremony on the street. I look out at a sea of faces, many streaked with tears: the children, grandchildren, and great-grandchildren of the perpetrators, my friends.

The Stolperstein project is made up of volunteers who assist in the historical research at the municipal archives, who comb through hundreds of deportation documents and police files, and who help raise the funds to install these markers. In doing so, they seek to make amends for their country's Nazi past and to educate current and future generations. By humanizing and personalizing the people who were humiliated, arrested, mistreated, robbed of their possessions, disowned, and finally herded together to be deported and murdered in the Holocaust, this project has become a trigger for new and intergenerational dialogue among the German people about the Nazi war crimes.

It is the Cologne artist Gunter Demnig, the son of a loyal Nazi SS man, who created these brass-plated cobblestones known as the *Stolpersteine*, German for stumbling stones. Wearing his signature brown suede wide-brimmed hat, earring stud, red scarf, and a much-needed vest for warmth, Gunter embeds the stones in the sidewalk in front of the doorway of the homes where the persecuted had once lived. Most of the victims are Jewish, but the stones also draw attention to the fate of gypsies, gay men and women, mentally and physically handicapped people, Jehovah's Witnesses, and political opponents of the Nazis.

Each simple memorial chronicles the person's life and death in its starkest details. The stones seem to be a metaphor for the Germans—that they not fall or trip but merely stumble over this horrific past with only their hearts. Driven by a passion to illuminate his country's past, Gunter has single-handedly embedded more than 53,000 such stones in over one thousand German cities and towns since hammering the first brass block into a Berlin sidewalk in 1996.

It haunts me that my parents each had to journey through the darkness alone. Now they are together again, their journey engraved onto the four-inch, brass-plated stone blocks that Gunter has embedded in the pavement of the house where my family once lived.

Here lived	Here lived
MALCHA GUTMANN	NATHAN GUTMANN
Born 1908	Born 1902
Fled 1938 France	Fled 1938 France
Deported 1942	Deported 1943
Murdered in	Murdered in
Auschwitz	Auschwitz

To open a book and read of six million slaughtered people is just an abstraction. I know how much more of an effect the unimaginable number of destroyed human beings has when we are faced with the personal destiny of just one family.

I hold my parents' wedding photograph high above my head and shout to the huge crowd of people, "I have brought my parents home. These *Stolpersteine* are their voice—Jews, who once lived, loved, had children and a normal happy life in this house. These stones are a reminder that my parents were neighbors who lived happily alongside other neighbors, until suddenly they disappeared, their apartment emptied and furniture taken away. And no one knew anything? The fact is that everyone just pretended to not know anything. There was never any question of where the Jews had gone and why."

"A person is only forgotten when his name has been forgotten," I shout out. "There are too many people who say we don't want to hear it anymore, but with these stones everybody sees that it did happen—in this neighborhood, in this house, in their apartment."

And now I know why the words that are imbedded in the ground next to the statue of Colonel Claus von Stauffenberg had touched me so deeply. Deciding not to take Herr Heilman's fear of skinheads marking graffiti on his house as a reason to stop my need to honor my parents was also a path to resistance. Every time Herr Heilman told his office staff that he was at a meeting, or on a holiday, or that he'd get back to me and never did, I refused to give up. These two *Stolpersteine* that have been embedded for my parents is how I had also fought for justice and honor.

Because there is no grave, I am condemned to go on mourning. And of course I know that these two *Stolpersteine* are not graves, they cannot be. Mama and Papa have gone up in smoke in Auschwitz, their ashes strewn into the river, yet in this solemn moment where I feel chilled and warmed, and both frightened and comforted at the same time, I remember the calm I always feel when I visit my beloved sister Rita's grave.

Something about these Stumbling Stones feels the same.

CHAPTER FORTY-SEVEN

EMPTY ROOMS

Frau Frankenstein has forwarded me an email from a man named Herr Platt. I speak a somewhat better German now thanks to the class I have attended for the last year, but I still ask Karola to translate this email for me.

September 12, 2007

Dear Mr. Demnig and the Stolperstein Initiative,

I help out occasionally to move furniture for a friend of mine who has a used furniture store in Prenzlauer Berg. Last week, a young woman called that she had some furniture that had belonged to her recently deceased grandmother (Anneliese Steinhardt) that she wished to dispose of on Raumerstrasse 21 here in Berlin.

Since I *stumbled* over the *Stolpersteine* several times while carrying down the individual pieces of furniture, I asked the young woman if her grandmother happened to know the Gutmann family.

She said no, but that it was the Gutmanns' apartment where her grandmother had lived for sixty-five years (since 1940?). My friend and I were quite taken aback by this. It is very unlikely that the apartment would have been unoccupied for two years after the family fled to France in 1938. We are quite certain that it was occupied and fully furnished, with all the belongings that the family was forced to leave behind.

It is quite possible that the furniture we were acquiring would have belonged to the Gutmann family. Might there be any surviving relatives of the Gutmanns who would be interested in it?

Perhaps you could put us in contact. Attached is a link to the furniture store and an e-mail address.

Best wishes and all the best of luck on your projects.

Tom Platt

* * *

September 15, 2007

Dear Tom,

I am the daughter of Nathan and Malcha Gutmann. I have lived in Berlin for the last five years, but I come from the USA. The *Stolpersteine* for my parents were laid in 2005. In 2004 I had tried in vain to find out in which apartment my family had actually lived. I could find nothing.

My two sisters had lived in this house, but I was born in Antwerp, Belgium, in 1939. Your email went deep into my heart. I cried. It is a miracle.

I live in Friedenau but in December I will move back to America. Please, please I want so much for us to meet. Call me. My number is 85 07 38 90.

My German is not that great, but I think you will be able to read my words. It was so kind of you to take the time to inquire about a living Gutmann relative.

You have given me an unforgettable gift.

With grateful greetings,

Sylvia Ruth Gutmann

* * *

Two days later I ride the *S-Bahn* to Prenzlauer Allee. I walk past the Penny discount store and the hardware store, where I stop to buy a small tube of the brass cleaner that I use to clean my parents' stones. Two blocks down, I see the familiar white street sign of Raumerstrasse. It always feels surreal to me that this is the same Raumerstrasse sign that my parents had seen too. No matter how many times I come to clean my parents' stones and visit with Herr Wassner and his lovely wife, I must stop to look at it.

But today I have no time to linger in front of the sign, for I am twenty minutes late and I cannot keep Tom Platt waiting any longer. I am running to the green house, the most beautiful house on this block, and even from halfway down the block I shout to Tom, "I'm sorry I'm so late." Tom had told me on the phone that he neither speaks nor does he understand English, yet his voice is soft and his German is clear and so uncomplicated that I can understand every word.

Tom rings Herr Wassner's buzzer, and holding my hand we walk together through the lobby of Raumerstrasse 21. Herr Wassner greets me with a warm and welcoming embrace, and together with Tom we walk up to the third floor. He opens the door of the apartment to my right.

Why am I being led into an old, empty apartment? I

wonder. I turn around to ask Herr Wassner but he is gone. This feels very strange and a little frightening.

"This is the apartment of the late Frau Steinhardt, and where my friend and I picked up the furniture for his used furniture store," Tom says. "It is being renovated. I believe that this was where your family lived."

I am stunned. I can't breathe. I feel my heart banging against my chest. I am dizzy and my stomach clenches. My brain hears Tom's words in slow motion, like a still in a movie.

Holding tightly onto Tom's hand, I walk into a large, high-ceilinged room. I imagine this room to be the kitchen. I picture the old stove, a small white fridge, and a pantry stocked with spices and jars of homemade jam. I see my family sitting around a long, wooden table eating lunch (*Mittagessen*), or celebrating a birthday or an anniversary, or lighting the candles with Mama to welcome in the Sabbath queen.

The old apartment is huge, with three windowed rooms on either side of a long, wide, high-ceilinged foyer. There in the smaller room I picture my two sisters: red-haired, five-year-old Rita and blond-haired, four-year-old Susi, playing with their dolls as they wait for their papa to come home from his weeklong trip selling hairbrushes and cosmetics in the nearby towns.

This room must be the living room where the family sat listening to the classical music my papa loved. Over there is my parents' bedroom with its king-size bed and carved, dark, wooden headboard and thick, goose down-filled pillows and comforter. And here is the bathroom with the old claw-footed bathtub and the toilet in the corner.

I run my hand along the walls of every room and the foyer too. I want to live here with them. I want to sit with my sisters around that long, wooden table and watch Mama light the Sabbath candles. I want to wait for my papa to come home and to run into his arms and be smothered with his kisses.

The room goes blurry. Tears trickle down my cheeks with my heart thudding wildly. Tom folds me in his arms. Home is no longer a place. It is buried under the ruins of my lost past. Standing here I feel like a stranger to myself. I feel the overwhelming absence of my family. Their whole world was brutally and systematically destroyed. I mourn for the child who should have lived in this apartment with them. "I want that life. Even for just a moment," I cry to Tom.

I make my way to the front door with Tom following behind me when he stops to reach into his pocket. He pulls out an old Swiss army knife and unscrews two long screws from the lock on the door. He removes the door lock with the original key still inside and silently lays it in my hand.

I cannot speak, so I just mouth a "thank you" and give him a quick embrace as we walk silently out to the street. We stand on the street as I always do when I'm here to take one more look at the house where my family had lived.

"Oh my God," I say, pointing to the windows of the apartment we just left. "Tom, on the day of the ceremony for the *Stolpersteine*, an old woman was hanging out of the window of this apartment. She was shouting to the crowd. I did not hear her at first because I too was shouting; there were so many people here. I remember shouting, 'With these stumbling stones I have brought my parents home.'

"But, I was frozen and in watcher mode when I finally heard her words. 'Again with the murdered Jews. These stones by the door are a terrible sight. What was so awful for the Jews in that time? Look, they are everywhere now. I have had enough of this old stuff.'

"My friends were trying so hard not to notice her, but it was impossible so they began to laugh. 'Look at the old battle-axe. What a foolish woman you are,' they shouted up to her."

"Well, good that she's dead," says a smiling Tom.

CHAPTER FORTY-EIGHT

FAMILY TIES

I am in the lobby of a nursing home in Antwerp, Belgium. It is the former Catholic hospital where I was born more than six decades ago. Next to the elevator hangs an old, enlarged photograph of a large, open room with rows of metal hospital beds and baby cribs. There are several nuns, each holding a tiny, swaddled newborn who must belong to each of the women pictured in the beds.

From there I follow the route on the map that Wendy, the lovely young director from the Antwerp Jewish Community Center, had drawn for me earlier in the day to the house where my family had lived. The house is ugly and rundown. Laundry hangs from the balconies, but I pray that in 1939 it had been sunny and clean, with flowerpots filled with brightly colored flowers sitting on the balcony. This is the house where my parents and sisters had lived and where they had brought me, their newly born daughter Ruth.

I have always wondered why my parents did not leave for America when they still could. Mama's brothers Sam and Herman had been in the States since 1935. Papa had his sisters Ella and Ida there too. My Daddy Sam owned a fur salon and his brother Herman had his union job as a printer working for a daily newspaper. I'm certain that Mama's brothers could have easily provided federal tax returns and bank statements that showed solid and steady monthly incomes. They would have gladly guaranteed that the prospective immigrants would not be a financial burden on America. I know they would have spent the hours and days and sometimes months that it took to file an Affidavit of Support and Sponsorship.

But it's not until I am in the Registrar's Office in Antwerp and the registrar gives me the file he had found on my family that I hear the cruel, heartbreaking answer. "Your parents had applied for visas to America," he says as he kindly translates the Flemish document for me. "Precious few refugees were allowed entry due to the National Origins Quota of 1924, and even though your parents were born in Germany, their parents were Polish, so your family was denied entry. The tiny quota of Polish immigrants allowed to enter the United States had been exhausted." *They could have lived.* I know it's hopeless to get so angry about something that happened more than seven decades ago, but now I want to scream at the America I love, "Your closeted fear and hatred for the Jew let my parents die!"

As I leaf through the seventeen-page, seventy-year-old Flemish document, I see the names Levy and Bertha Gutmann. This must be the man that my two sisters called Uncle Paldo, my father's brother, and his wife, but I don't understand what he is doing in this Belgian document. I plead with the busy but kind registrar to translate one more page for me.

"Levy and Bertha fled Germany to Antwerp, Belgium, in 1938," he translates. "In the summer of 1942 they were arrested and shipped to the Malines transit camp. Levy Gutmann, born May 7, 1897, in Berlin, Germany, perished in Auschwitz on

July 31, 1943. Bertha Gutmann, born May 5, 1899, in Basel, Switzerland, perished in Auschwitz on August 2, 1943," he solemnly says.

On gray sheets of French, German, and Flemish archival papers that list convoy numbers and deportation dates, where their journey of death ends is how I meet the family I never knew. Fragments of lives unlived.

* * *

It is a frozen, dark Berlin morning in December 2007. Two years after the laying of my parents' stumbling stones, Gunter has laid four more *Stolpersteine* for my family. On the night of October 28, 1938, some seventeen thousand Polish Jews, including my paternal grandparents Markus and Chawa Gutmann and my maternal grandparents Rifka and Naftali Kleinman, were expelled from Germany and forced across the border to Poland. Poland refused to allow the Jews entry, and with no food or water the deportees remained stranded and left to die of the cold and starvation in the no-man's land between Germany and Poland near the town of Zbaszyn. Grandfather Markus was a deeply religious man who spent his life studying Torah. Grandmother Chawa wore a wig to cover her hair in modesty, owned a candy store, and was a *balabusta*, the Yiddish word for mistress of the house, and good homemaker. Zbaszyn was where my sixty-nine-year-old grandfather and his sixty-seven-year-old wife were lined up with the other Polish refugees and gunned down by an SS firing squad in 1938.

My grandmother was only a year older than I am now. Were my grandparents allowed to hold hands and stand next to each other? I wonder. Were they allowed a last embrace? Did they plead to the God they loved to show himself and save them? Or did they cry out, "Why have you deserted us?" As part of the permanent exhibit in the Holocaust Memorial Museum in Washington, DC, they have on display an old black-and-white photo of an SS firing squad with cigarettes hanging from the men's lips and laughing as they fire away. I pray that my frightened, helpless, gentle grandparents and the hundreds of other Jewish Polish refugees were spared that indignity the day they were shot and thrown into the pile of bodies in an open ditch.

* * *

A hundred people, bundled and layered from head to toe, are gathered around me on Barnimstrasse 38 in Berlin. Number 38 is now a seven-story high-rise with an elevator (it is rare to find an elevator in the older buildings). It is an ugly, box-like white building that looks just like all the buildings the Russians built after the war. Number 38 is where Papa's parents Markus and Chawa lived.

Cantor Ehrenburg from the Pestalozzistrasse synagogue is here, and with a voice that sounds like Luciano Pavarotti's, he sings the Kaddish, the Hebrew prayer for the dead. I look out at the hundred people who have gathered on Barnimstrasse to commemorate Chawa and Markus with two new stumbling stones that Gunter Demnig has embedded into the pavement.

Frau Sigrid Klebba, the district head of Youth, Family, and Sports for Friedrichshain-Kreuzberg—the district where my grandparents lived—stands by my side and speaks to the group. I smile and nod, pretending that I understand. Although I speak and understand German much better thanks to the class I have attended for the last year, Frau Klebba speaks too fast and in a different dialect than I am used to hearing, so there are only one or two phrases I can catch. I hear her say that Frau Gutmann is giving us the gift of these memorial stones to remember our past, and that we must use that past to help build a better future. And something about a museum and an American teacher named Ken Brown. I will ask my expat American friend Ariel to tell me about the parts of the speech I did not understand.

My forty-year-old son David is not here. Divorced, and fired from yet another junior accounting job, he is angry, depressed, and broke. Unwilling to let me pay for a round-trip ticket to Berlin, he refuses to be part of this event that means so much to me.

Because it has only been two years since my sister Susi was here for Mama and Papa's commemoration, and although it had been a surprisingly nice experience for her to come back to Berlin, the city where she was born, she did not wish to come this time. "Once is enough," she answers when I call.

This former East Berlin neighborhood was bombed and destroyed by the Allies. Now there is a huge Kaiser's supermarket where number 18 once stood. Papa's brother Levy and his wife Bertha lived there.

"Ariel," I whisper, "please tell me what Frau Klebba said. Who is Ken Brown and why did she talk about a museum?"

"Ken Brown teaches German and economics at Alcoa High School in Alcoa, Tennessee," Ariel translates. "When he was a young student he spent several months in Germany. He fell in love with the language so he taught himself to speak German." Wow, I think. It has taken a year of German language class and the German friends I love for me not to hear it as the language of the murderers.

"Searching for a project that would involve both the Alcoa School and the seniors in his German language class, he remembered an article he read about the *Stolpersteine* in an old newsletter he'd tucked away. He found the website where he read that for 120 Euro anyone could sponsor a stone. He knew this would be the perfect project when he read that the *Stolpersteine* in front of the buildings where they are installed bring back to memory the people who once lived there. That each stone begins with HERE LIVED—One stone, one name, one person."

So this is the American school that Frau Bauer, the new director of the Stumbling Stone Initiative, told me about. And Ken Brown teaches there, I realize.

"Ken Brown's class donated the 120 Euro for each of your grandparents' stones," Ariel explains. "The Friedrichshain-Kreuzberg Museum had offered to broadcast the ceremony, which the whole school is watching right now back in Tennessee."

Frau Bauer and her crew of volunteers have spent months researching the archives to gather the information that Gunter will carve onto the new brass stones. "In the past two years we have built a wonderful English language website," Frau Bauer tells me. "The site has been hugely successful, and people love this project and want to be part of it, and the donations keep pouring in. I am happy that the *Stolpersteine* project will pay for the four stones that you are having laid. As I told you earlier, the senior class at the Alcoa School has paid for your grandparents' stones. Levy Gutmann's stone was paid for by two well-known Hamburg TV film producers. The stone for Levy's wife Bertha was paid for by the class in the Berlin Kolleg, where you have spoken many times."

Mr. Ken Brown, you will be my first phone call when I get home to America next month, I promise.

But on this frozen December morning the crowds of people start to break up and walk down to the corner for the second ceremony of the two Stumbling Stones that Gunter has embedded on Barnimstrasse 18 for Levy and Bertha Gutmann, Papa's brother and his wife. Just as I am about to join the crowd and Cantor Ehrenberg walking down to the corner, I hear someone calling my name.

"Frau Gutmann?"

I turn to the small, round man who stands before me at number 38. "My name is Herr Müller. I am so sorry but I do not speak English," he says.

"No problem," I assure him in German. "We will manage."

"I read a story about you in the local paper," he says. "That you were having this stumbling stone commemoration for your grandparents today. I had left this neighborhood more than fifty years ago and have only recently moved back. I knew that God had given me the paper to read—for I have never read it before—so that I could be here with you today." *When he refers to God, I know that I am about to hear something startling.*

"I lived in number 38 as a child and once a week I'd go to your grandmother's candy shop on the ground floor to buy candy, but she always gave me a big handful for free. I was playing with my friends outside when I saw your grandmother and grandfather—each holding a small suitcase, each dressed in black, your grandmother's skirt hung down to her shoes, your grandfather with his long beard and black coat and big, black-fur brimmed hat—being led to the corner to a big covered truck by the two SS men on either side of them. I was very frightened. I did not know what was happening so I ran to my apartment to tell my mother about what I had just seen, but she smacked me and warned me to never speak of this again. I was only seven years old."

I can't remember who is holding onto whom at this point. We are both in tears. A large crowd surrounds us when he says, "This secret has lain inside of me like a rock for sixty years, but today I meet the granddaughter from America who has set me free."

Another profoundly moving, magical shift happens for me today. Two people are forever bound by a moment spent on a narrow, dead-end street, in front of the house where my grandparents had once lived.

With the laying of these four stones, I have returned my family back to the city they loved and called home. Having lost my home, for me "home" is still a foreign place; when I am here I want to be somewhere else. And maybe it will always be this way, but for now I too will return to America, the place I love and call home.

I see that the distance I traveled for love was not only the four thousand miles to be with Jannek; I also traveled sixty years into the past. I have found a loving, generous circle of German friends. Looking for my parents has planted my roots firmly in the ground. Not until I lived in Berlin could I finally see myself without all the trappings of self-pity and rage. I am raw and naked; making my way back to the woman I'd been before I learned the art of disguise. And in the end—in the place I feared the most—I end up meeting the person it was always worth changing for: myself.

I feel the presence of everyone who has ever believed in me and who offered me his or her love. They have strengthened my wholeness and my true identity. Their love is always with me even if it was long ago. How ironic that the anguished legacy of the Holocaust and all the loss has made me strong and confident. The Germans have set me free. Becoming transparent feels to me like I've been peeling an onion, layer by layer by layer.

CHAPTER FORTY-NINE

PAPER CLIPS

January 2008. I am home in America and living with my forty-one-year-old son David in the two-bedroom apartment in Dallas where he lived with his ex-wife. He has only four more semesters to complete in order to graduate with a bachelor's degree in accounting. I will use my Social Security and the monthly German pension that the Office of Reparations wires to my bank to pay the rent, food, and all our expenses.

I commit to stay for the nine months until he graduates in August, but then I will go to New York and stay with my friend until I find a place of my own.

* * *

A month later I fly to Tennessee, where the entire senior class, and a tall, handsome, smiling man with open arms welcome me at the Knoxville airport. "Hello, Sylvia. So glad you came to share your story with us," shouts Ken in a booming southern drawl. The students have arranged the weekend. We will visit places of interest in and around the Alcoa School. A pizza party is in full swing at one student's home that night. The following day I will speak to Ken's senior class and the Blount Middle School.

The room is filled with fifteen-year-old students from the Blount High School. I stand on a raised platform holding onto a microphone. The students sit on blue-painted, concrete, bench-like seats three levels high. A pretty, dark-haired woman sits beside me on the stage. She is an American Sign Language interpreter. Because I have less than an hour with these young students, I take only twenty minutes to share my story. I end with these words: "One story puts a human face on the immense, unimaginable loss. One murder is not a statistic, but a loved one." As I have always done in Berlin, it is more important to leave time for the students to share their stories with the group and me.

She has short, curly, blond hair and wears a T-shirt, long shorts, and sneakers. She beams a wide smile as she firmly grips the microphone I hand her. She looks like she has a lot to say. Her nametag reads Ivy. When she begins to talk, the manner of her speech tells me that she is hearing impaired. "I got very sad when you told us that your family was murdered just because they were Jewish," Ivy says. It is difficult to understand her. "How ugly and cruel of the people who picked on your family because they did not have blond hair and blue eyes. They were still God's children. I know how bad it feels to be different."

Oh, oh, what could have happened to this pretty, smiling, fifteen-year-old student to make her feel this way? I feel the tears rising, so I take a long sip of water to prevent them from spilling out. Lucy, the sign-language interpreter, takes the mic from Ivy who proceeds to sign. "The kids make fun of me and call me names because I dress like a boy," Lucy interprets. "They call me dumb because I'm deaf. They laugh at me when I talk." Tears are running down my blush-streaked cheeks. Lucy is choking back tears as she shares Ivy's words. The young teacher is staring at the floor.

"But, I don't care what they call me or what they say," Ivy continues signing. "I'm happy just the way I am." The room is still. It feels eerie, as if no one is even breathing. These young people look like they are in a trance.

Ivy turns to walk back to her seat, but I grab her hand and silently mouth, "Stay."

"Did you know how Ivy felt?" I ask the crowd. "Does making fun of Ivy make you feel better about yourselves? Does shaming Ivy lessen your own shame? Does making Ivy feel small make you feel big?"

I am looking at Ivy, who is looking at her pretty signer, when I notice a small tear in the corner of Ivy's eye. Then I see the students rising, rushing to the stage. With outstretched black arms, brown arms, white arms, and tattooed arms, they gather around Ivy in a huge communal hug.

Everyone is laughing and crying and shouting, "We love you, Ivy."

* * *

I am the guest of honor at a candle-lighting ceremony. I am deeply touched when Ken tells me that he contacted the Tennessee Holocaust Commission to ask about this ceremony. The survivors of the Holocaust light six candles in honor of the six million who perished, on Yom HaShoah, Holocaust Remembrance Day. But there are seven candles on the table tonight. The first candle is lit in memory of the political prisoners who were tortured and killed. The next candle is lit to remember the homosexuals who perished in the camps. The next candle is lit in memory of the gypsies who died in the camp. The next candle is lit in memory of the Jehovah's

Witnesses who perished. The next candle is lit to remember the six million Jews who perished. I light the sixth candle in memory of the million and a half children who perished. The seventh candle is lit for the five million men, women, and children who have not been accounted for.

On the last day of my Alcoa visit we go on a field trip to Whitwell, Tennessee, and the famous Paperclip Museum. Whitwell Middle School Principal Linda Hooper asked the language arts teacher, Sandra Roberts, and Associate Principal David Smith to begin a Holocaust education class. It would be the basis for teaching tolerance and diversity in a voluntary after-school program in this small, rural community of fewer than two thousand people nestled in the mountains of Tennessee. When the mostly white and Christian students struggled to grasp the concept and the enormity of the six million Jews who died during the Holocaust, they decided to collect six million paper clips—one for each soul who perished.

"Why did they use paper clips?" I ask the student docent.

"When we researched this project, we learned that the Norwegian people had worn a paper clip on their clothing in silent protest, a symbol of resistance against the Nazi occupation."

This simple paper clip project idea eventually turned into a worldwide phenomenon. It drew international media attention and letters of support from every continent.

In 2001, the school dedicated a Children's Holocaust Memorial inside an authentic German rail car that was used to transport the victims to labor and death camps. The young docent tells me that this car was part of the *Reichsbahn* and one of the last remaining cattle cars of the Nazi era.

I am frozen and hold my breath. I cannot move at the sight of this cattle car. It looks like the one I saw with Uri when we visited the memorial in Drancy, France. How desperately I clawed at the locked door, wanting to get inside, but now I am too frightened to walk inside.

Then I look around and see a field of butterflies. Stained-glass butterflies, free-standing copper sculptured butterflies, and colorful paper butterflies flap their wings in the wind on sticks, a hundred butterflies planted in the ground surrounding the car. Because of the butterfly I saw on the windowsill on the day when my beloved sister Rita died, they have become a symbol of freedom and renewal for me. I am safe.

The rail car houses 11 million paper clips in a huge glass jar, one for each victim of the Holocaust. There are more than thirty thousand letters in every language. A large collection of Holocaust survivor books lines the shelves. A small monument honors the millions of children lost in the Holocaust. These young Christian students of the Whitwell Middle School, many of whom may not have ever even met a Jew, have transformed this former death car into a symbol of renewed life, honoring the millions of lives that were lost.

For generations of Whitwell students, a paper clip will never again be just a paper clip. Instead, the paper clip is a reminder of the importance of perseverance, empathy, tolerance, and understanding.

Ken drives me to the airport for my trip back to Dallas. We are good friends, Ken and I, and from then on, every year I will fly to Tennessee to share my story of hope and the power of forgiveness with the new seniors in Ken's German studies class. Ken will travel to Berlin every two years with a new senior class to visit my family's stones. The students bring a bouquet of red roses that they lay on the stones, and then they hold hands and make a circle surrounding the stones as Ken leads them in a prayer.

* * *

"David, you promised to take your big exercise machines out of that second bedroom while I was gone. I need my own room. I have no privacy in the living room, and that old sofa bed hurts my back."

"I said I'd get to it, Mom," he mutters back. "Don't keep bothering me about this."

Stay calm, Sylvia, I think, but I can't hold down how angry and disappointed I feel, so I shout back, "You're so unwilling to do anything for me. Why is that, David?"

David just shrugs and rolls his eyes, and in the midst of my fury he walks to his bedroom and shuts the door. I have been dismissed. I'm furious. I feel trapped by my promise. I know I'll be sleeping on that old sofa bed in the living room for the next five months. I need some air, so I walk to Borders bookstore, where I sit at an empty table, my tears spilling onto my carrot cake.

Early on I had made myself the guardian of David's well being. Because his father had abandoned him, I held on even tighter to him. I was his voice. I was his protector. I had to fight for him. If more than three days had passed and I didn't hear his voice, I was convinced that he was in the hospital, or worse yet, dead. I can't remember when this dark scenario started. Probably the moment I could no longer keep a watchful eye on him every waking hour. For years I've tiptoed around my only child, so as not to anger him. I creep around David's moods.

I am vigilant, careful, and appeasing. I'm always the one to apologize. I make nice. I bring calm to his righteous, arrogant, angry outbursts. I stuff down my feelings, my instincts, and more importantly my boundaries, just to hear him say, "Not only are you my mother, you're my best friend." I lap it up like a dog waiting to be patted on the head. *Good girl.*

Although my life is rich, it is also dominated by the dark shadow of the Holocaust. My childhood experience has certainly shaped my life. Now I must face the truth. I am still in the grips of, and hostage to, this compulsive, insatiable hunger I have to be needed and loved. I have a hole inside that I've tried to fill with food, with men, with friends, and with my son. I cannot fill it. I cannot conquer this demon. I am not enough for my son, so I must buy his love. Plain me, without an offering of my money and time, is a foreign concept to me.

"Go ahead," David shouts while I nervously pack my bags. "Get out."

David drives me in silence to a seedy motel near the airport. I will stay until my flight to New York leaves the next day. "I'm sorry," I start, but he tells me to get out of the car. I am sobbing as I watch him drive away. *What have I done? Was I wrong to leave?* Questions I grapple with all night.

With only an hour's sleep I'm feeling fragile and vulnerable. *I have lost my son. I may never see him again.* As I wait in the Dallas airport for my flight to New York, I keep hearing David shout, "Get out."

And, there it is, the boogeyman. Rita's early warning. Be a good girl or they will tell you to get out too.

The deepest feeling known to me is the sense of not belonging. I grew up with that feeling. That Gerdy would just be happier without me. She did not love me. That really no one can love me. That is my greatest fear; that I am left all alone.

Rita, with her words that she spoke with love and care, would have never wished for me to be burdened with this lifelong dread. I am finally face to face with my deepest fears: being abandoned, unloved, and alone. The Holocaust has impacted the most intimate and fragile part of me.

And, now I wonder. *Has the shrapnel, which exploded from the Holocaust that has impacted me, impacted David too? Did I hold onto him too tightly? Was I over-protective? Was I too involved in his life? Did I suffocate him with my insatiable need for love? Did I expect too much, or not enough?*

"You were a great mom," he'd say. "I remember when you went to the Board of Education building and you marched into that office demanding that I be put into a special-ed class and not the class for retarded children. How you sacrificed so many years working three jobs to pay for my tutors and therapy sessions. How you refused to have me take Ritalin and found the Feingold Diet instead."

David was always praising me. But, maybe behind his awe of my courage and strength, there is really guilt and shame. Maybe, like I once felt, he too feels less than. Maybe my resilience and my courage have inhibited him? Maybe he thinks that nothing he does could ever match up?

While my early trauma could have been passed down to my son, so too could my resilience. No, I will not go back. I have had enough. I am done with rescuing, caretaking, and enabling my son. I will let go. No more will I meddle or offer him unsolicited advice.

My sister Rita was my place. I never had to worry that she would not take me in, no matter what. I think I have tried doing that with David, but it never worked. When we live together David is belligerent and disrespectful and takes me for granted, but I forgot that. I was wrong to have promised David, without thinking it through, that I would stay for nine months and pay his rent and all the expenses so that he could go to school.

It will take a long time, and maybe forever, for this to blow over. I know my son. He's angry. He has always counted on me to solve his problems, be they emotional or financial. He's frightened now that he won't make it on his own.

I pray that David will find his own way. He has good bones under that thin skin. He comes from good stock. A year later he finally calls. Our conversations are always about him.

CHAPTER FIFTY

A VOYAGE OF THE HEART

As I wait for my friend Jean, in whose apartment I now stay, until I find a place of my own, I open my computer and check my emails. When I open the one from my German friend Conny, there is no text. All I see on the screen is a dark, grainy photograph of a group of children. In the first row sit one boy and four young girls. In the second row stand four girls and two tall boys. In the last row, wearing berets, stand five boys, five girls, and a young woman whose face is only partially visible under her white nurse's cap.

Why has Conny sent me this picture? I quickly email to ask her. I get no immediate response and I am so anxious to know, but then I look at my watch and realize that in Germany it is three in the morning.

The next day, after a sleep-disrupted night, as soon as Jean leaves, I look at my emails. "The photo was taken in Camp Rivesaltes," Conny writes. "I copied it from Lisl Hanau's memoir. She is the eighteen-year-old nurse in the picture. She is eighty-three years old now and she lives in Jerusalem." Who is Lisl Hanau?

I stare at the screen at this ensemble of children in the French internment camp where 2,251 foreign-born Jews, including 110 children and my mother, had been interned and deported to Auschwitz.

"Rita, it's you!" I shout. It is my ten-year-old sister in the second row. I continue searching through the faces; the photo is quite grainy, but now I see the half-hidden face of my nine-year-old sister Susi in the last row. I am anxious; I hear nothing but the sound of my nervous breath, yet I am also guardedly excited so I continue my search. One little girl in the first row has short, dark hair and a moon-pie face; her bangs skim the top of her eyebrows. Her legs are bare, and she wears a jacket or maybe it is a short coat. She looks to be the youngest child in the group. It's hard to make out her features so I lean closer to the screen.

Even in this grainy, sixty-five-year-old, black-and-white photograph, her eyes are too vacant for a three-year-old.

"Oh my God! It's me. It's me!" The three-year-old self I had left behind in the camp. I have only two photographs of myself as a child. One is the photo I had sent to Madeleine in 1999, where Papa is holding me up when I was two, and the other was taken after being smuggled into Switzerland with my sisters, when I was four.

My sister only remembered Mademoiselle Rothschild. The only memory that Rita could share about our time in the camp was when I broke from the line and cried for Mama to take me, and when the French guards shoved Mama into the cattle car. At the end of the story, Rita always whispered, "It was the last time I would see Mama." Even when she smiled and radiated happiness, I saw that sad, sad moment in Rita's eyes. Through all the years I spent in Rita's Cleveland kitchen, her with a chunk of German salami in one hand and the end piece of freshly baked seeded rye bread in the other, she never told me about a nurse named Lisl Hanau.

When I asked her, "Rita, why did we not go with Mama?" she'd answer, "Maybe on the day that Mama left, the Vichy guards had told the parents they could leave their children behind." Whenever I share my story, this part of the story always sounds like a fairy tale and impossible to believe. Everything tells me that the Vichy police had never shown this kindness before. Now I will finally learn the truth.

I write back, "Conny, I must go to Israel. Maybe Lisl will remember my mama? Maybe she will remember me?"

Having found the picture, Conny will meet me in Israel. A documentary filmmaker, she has gone to Auschwitz with me and has also filmed all of the events where I have spoken in Berlin. Sadly, it is not optioned by the German television station as she had hoped it would be.

She will film this memorable time with Lisl and me, and hopes to sell it to the long-awaited Rivesaltes Memorial project. Conny makes all the arrangements and pays for the ticket that I use to fly to Israel to begin the most important trip of my life.

***

Today I will meet Lisl Hanau, the nurse who saved me. I am told that she is excited to meet one of the children left in her care.

It is an unusually cool and windy April day in 2008 when I enter the lobby of the Dere'h Hebron seniors residence in Jerusalem. "It's on the third floor, to the left of the elevator, the last door next to the window at the end of the hallway," the receptionist instructs Conny and me. I knock on the door but no one answers, so I knock again. No one comes, so I try turning the doorknob, and when I open the door I see a small, gray-haired woman in a red sweater, sitting in an armchair.

She gets up and walks to the door shouting, "Sylvie?"

My throat closes as I try to speak, so I just nod yes, and I bury my face in her outstretched arms. My tears burst forth like a dam released. They wet her glasses. My now-crushing embrace has set off her old hearing aid and it's beeping loudly in her ear, but I am unable to release her. I want to crawl into her skin.

"*Wie alt ist dieses Kind?*" Lisl asks. How old is this child?

"Sixty-nine," I answer.

"Yes, I thought so," she says.

It is hard for me to wrap my head around this moment. I am really in Israel, in the small, neat apartment of the woman that I saw in that old, grainy photograph. It feels otherworldly that I am really embracing the young nurse in the photograph I had seen on my computer screen. It feels like I am in a movie.

We are standing in her tiny bedroom, where her past and present life hang on the wall near her bed: framed pictures of her late husband, her parents, her early nursing degree, the Strasbourg house where she lived with her parents, her nine grandchildren, and her thirteen-year-old great-grandchild. Pointing to the picture of her adult son, an only child, she says, "He is a doctor in Strasbourg. I used to visit him quite often, but because my vision and hearing have deteriorated I can no longer travel. When he is able to take time away from his practice he comes and visits me. My son is very good to me. He found this wonderful place for me."

I put her hand on my heart, overcome with gratitude and love and barely able to speak. "I also have a son because you saved me."

"Come, little one," Lisl says. Holding my hand, she tells me to sit with her at the kitchen table, and hands me a paper napkin to dry my face.

"I was eighteen in 1942 and had just completed my nursing studies," Lisl begins. "I was working in a Jewish nursing home in Strasbourg, France, when I received an urgent call from Andrée Salomon, the director of the *Oeuvre de Secours aux Enfants,* the Organization to Save the Children. 'Take the train tonight and join me in Camp Rivesaltes,' she demanded. 'You will be the official nurse of the children's barrack.'

"'It will be difficult for me to leave so soon,' I replied.

"'Do not forget to pack long underwear and a toothbrush.' When Mademoiselle Salomon gave an order, one did not disobey.

"Camp Rivesaltes is a vast encampment of wooden barracks spread out over three kilometers of an open, stony plain, not far from the Mediterranean. I do not see a blade of grass anywhere in the camp. It had been a military camp thirty years earlier, but now it was being used to house the Central European Jews, mostly women and children. They have either been rounded up or caught trying to cross the Pyrenees into Spain, or they are turned away at the border when they try to enter Switzerland.

"People live with total lack of hygiene; the toilets are merely wooden planks, outside, without doors or walls. They sleep on lice-infested straw or straw-covered planks with just a rag for covering. In the barracks, there are no tables or chairs and no water in which to bathe or wash. Separated from the women and children, the men are idle and mentally distressed. Children are confined to their own barrack and only allowed a brief daily visit with their parents.

"The camp is surrounded by barbed wire, with a direct railroad connection, making Camp Rivesaltes the perfect place for the French Vichy government to imprison all these foreign-born Jews. The *indésirables!* The undesirables. The French guards are very anti-Semitic, and the internees are forbidden to practice their religion.

"Old people are dying of typhus and starvation. Babies are born but die soon after. Their mothers have no milk in the breast. Even the sick have to walk 150 meters to an outdoor water pump. The children are covered with lice. They get only milk coffee with no bread in the morning and rotten tomato soup for lunch with nothing more to eat until the following day."

Rita never skipped over the soup when she'd tell me the sad story of Rivesaltes. I still do not eat tomato soup.

"We have glacial winds in winter and torrid heat in summer. The wind whirls dust through the camp in gusts of up to 120 kilometers an hour. We have no running water, so I must walk to the water closet outside and use an old rag. I walk back to the barrack to wash and delouse the children's tiny, malnourished bodies. I work tirelessly taking care of my charges. I try to cheer them up and make them sing.

"When I am able to leave the camp I go to Perpignan where Paul Cerrazi, a devout and sympathetic Christian Vichy police chief, lives. He provided me with false papers showing me to be Christian, and supplied me the same forged identification papers for the children.

"Our objective is simple: avoid at all costs the deportation of the children to the death camps.

"Several months go by before I see that the situation in the camp is getting worse. Deportations are taking place at an accelerated pace. Now I go every night from barrack to barrack. 'Leave your children with me,' I beg their parents. 'I will keep them safe until your return.'" As I listen to Lisl, I feel dizzy and anxious and my heart is beating in my throat. The blood has drained from my face and my eyes are rimmed in red and they hurt. I think that I might not recover from hearing Lisl's wrenching tale of the French camp where my mother, my two sisters, and I were interned. Will it be too horrific and tragic to hear of the pain and loss I suffered? I worry that it will provoke an avalanche of emotion that could bury me. I fear that the despair and sorrow I feel will unleash my monstrous rage. Am I brave enough to live with these scenes forever in my head?

Thankfully, Lisl begs to stop. She has had enough for one day. I can see that even though all these events happened long ago, her memories of these events are still so vivid that it pains and disturbs her to relive them. For Lisl, Rivesaltes did not happen sixty-five years ago; it happened just a minute ago. Especially painful is to retell the tragedy *to one of her children*, as she refers to those she saved. She is tired. She needs to nap.

I promise to come back in the morning, but before I leave I ask, "What may I bring you?"

"Just your smile," Lisl answers.

This is such a simple reply from the woman who kept my two sisters and me in her care after Mama was shipped to Auschwitz. How meager my gift of a smile will be compared to the gift of life she gave me.

This is what really happened, not the version that Rita had shared with me. *Maybe on the day that Mama was deported the Vichy guards let the parents leave their children behind*, Rita would say. It was really Lisl who had begged Mama to leave her daughters behind, to save us. I am overwhelmed and stunned! All these years later, listening to Lisl's story has given me a glimpse into that day. My mother in her barrack hearing Lisl's pleas: *Leave your children with me!* I picture my young mother frightened, and heartbroken, in that dark, airless cattle car to Auschwitz crowded with its human cargo, and I pray that Mama knew that Lisl would save our lives. I want to believe this.

After all the sleuthing and digging for clues of what I thought was finally a full-circle journey, here is the information that has eluded me all these years. Lisl Hanau has given me the missing piece of the puzzle. Lisl *is* the missing piece.

* * *

Early the following morning I wait outside until Yad Vashem, the Holocaust museum in Jerusalem, opens. It is not far from the hotel where Conny and I stayed and the old people's home where Lisl lives. I hoped that by coming very early I could avoid the large crowd of tourists that has already gathered. I will have to come back another time to view all the exhibits. Today there is only one I must see before my visit with Lisl later in the day.

"Whoever Saves One Life—Saves the World Entire" is inscribed on the large stone wall where I enter the Garden of Righteous Among the Nations in Yad Vashem. It is so peaceful here in this lush and beautifully landscaped garden that is dedicated with its plaques and tablets to Righteous Gentiles, non-Jewish men and women who risked their lives to save a

Jew. Each marble tablet represents a country and lists the names of the rescuers from that country.

I look for the tablet marked "France." I find his name: Paul Cerrazi. It is near the top of the list. I put my lips on his name and thank this French police chief in Perpignan, who risked being found out and went against everything his Vichy government stood for to give French Christian identities to Lisl and her Jewish children.

* * *

"Come, come Sylvie, we must first eat," Lisl urges when I open her apartment door. I dare not say that I have already eaten breakfast, so I sit down beside her.

Lisl begins her story again. "From early morning on, the interned—a collection of men, women, and children—stand outside of their barracks. On the plaza in front of them is a raised platform for the French camp personnel. The interned listen with pounding hearts as the names of those who must leave boom from the loudspeakers. They move, one after the other, to the other side of the plaza to join the people who have already gathered for deportation. When I see the children standing next to the parents whose names are called, I go quickly to their side. We are forbidden to speak, so I say nothing. They know me; I visit with them at night. I tell them about the morning roll call and the transport, and I ask them to leave their children behind. 'Don't take them with you,' I beg. 'Push them into my waiting arms.'

"The parents are not even allowed a short hug with their children before I take them back to their barrack. Then I return to the roll call until the end of the day. They are tragic moments, but also ones of strength. The goal is as clear to the parents as it is to me: save the children.

"So many parents refused to separate themselves from their little ones, but today the children's barrack is full. Hope is on our side. We must act quickly. Madame Salomon, the OSE, and I will take care of them and, God willing, one day parent and child will find each other again."

At one point Lisl leaves the room for a moment, and when she comes back she is holding a red photo album in her hands. She opens the album and, holding a large magnifying glass, she points to the original of the photograph that I had seen on my computer screen three months earlier. I point at the little girl who is sitting on the ground, wearing a coat so small that her legs are bare. She has sad, sad eyes; I show her that it is me.

I have always hungered for a link to the past, for my family, destroyed connections, and a trace of me buried in a childhood that I could not remember. "This photograph is an unbelievable gift," I whisper. "It is solid proof that I had really been where I had been. It is a precious fragment from a shattered life."

"Cameras were forbidden in the camp, but several years ago I received this rare photograph from one of the boys in the picture," Lisl says. My heart begins to race when I imagine myself meeting this boy. Even if he were twelve in this photo, he would only be seventy-eight today. Maybe he remembers my mama, my sisters, and me. I'm excited about this imagined meeting, but then I hear Lisl say, "I do not remember which boy it was. Of all the children I saved, you are the first child that I have allowed to come and visit me. I have had no contact with them; these are the children I had walked back to the barrack after their parents were deported."

Lisl has taken me back to the day my mother left me. Waves of grief cross my face. It's hard to catch my breath. This is the story of that day in Rivesaltes.

I close my eyes to try and picture our mama the way Rita has always told me she looked. Mama with her red hair, porcelain skin, and fine bones was not only a fashion plate in the best of times when it was easy, but more importantly in the absolutely worst and most horrible time—the three years after I was born. Mama always managed somehow, with no more than the two suitcases my parents carried when they fled Berlin with Rita and Susi, to look as if she was going out with Papa to an expensive restaurant.

How horribly wrong, I think. That all the running, all the planning, all the looking chic and elegant to keep up an appearance of normalcy, all the begging and pleading for a night, a week, or a year or two to hide and be allowed to live— none of it saved our parents in the end.

I wish my sister Rita could have shared this memorable time with Lisl and me. How sad I am that Rita, who was so deserving of goodness, joy, and a long, happy life, has died. It was a long and cruel good-bye. I love Rita with a love that has dimmed little as the years have passed, and today she is more alive in me than ever before.

Not until this moment with Lisl do I *feel* my brave mother's ultimate gift of love. Mama had made a heart-wrenching choice—she gave me life again. But, maybe Mama was not the only one to make a decision that day. In this solemn moment I finally understand that subconsciously I made a silent promise to my mother that I would never be fully happy—it would be disloyal to Mama's sacrifice if I lived too well, became too rich or successful and lived with abundance. I know that it was completely irrational of me to have thought that the promise I made would have changed anything. Living with the guilt that I had been spared, I spent half my life with the belief that I had not earned that life. *Forgive me, Mama. Forgive me,* I silently cry, over and over again.

Upon my arrival in America at age seven I had lost my parents, my name, my language, my home, and my childhood. I grew up surrounded by a conspiracy of silence that said, "Put all that behind you. You have to erase from your memory everything that happened to you. You have to move on. Hide your pain." I was forced to give up my history and my past and told to keep my feelings and my anguish to myself.

It was crazy making, and why I always returned to that Camp Rivesaltes scene—because in my imagination it is that sad, traumatized, lost little girl that I search for. She is always part of the landscape that I visit. And today Lisl has made that day come alive. It has never been as vivid and potent to me as today. She has confirmed that experience for me—and reunited me with the child whose memory is completely lost to me. Lisl has helped me to reconcile pieces of myself that have never felt complete or whole.

My visit has nearly come to an end when suddenly I receive in my silenced memory the echo of the child I had been in the camp. Just as in Nay when I had a memory of the fountain in the park where I had played with my papa, here with Lisl I now sense a tiny piece of chocolate in the palm of my hand. I ask Lisl if this means anything.

"Yes," she answers. "When the children became separated from their parents they would scream in terror and despair when I'd walk them back to their barrack. As a way of offering comfort to the children who were left in my care, I'd place a tiny piece of chocolate in their hand."

* * *

One of my favorite passages reflecting the agony and the ecstasy of my life's journey is from *The Velveteen Rabbit*, by Margery Williams. In the story, two nursery toys, the Skin Horse and the Rabbit, talk about becoming Real:

"Does it hurt?" asked the Rabbit.

"Sometimes," said the Skin Horse, for he was always truthful. "When you are Real, you don't mind being hurt."

"Does it happen all at once, like being wound up," he asked, "or bit by bit?"

"It doesn't happen all at once," said the Skin Horse. "You become. It takes a long time. That's why it doesn't often happen to people who break, or have sharp edges, or have to be carefully kept. Generally, by the time you are Real, most of your hair has been loved off, and your eyes drop out and you get loose in the joints and very shabby. But these things don't matter at all, because once you are Real you can't be ugly, except to people who don't understand."

PHOTOGRAPHS

Mama and Papa's Wedding

Papa's Letter (page 1)

Papa's Letter (page 2)

Papa's Letter (page 3)

Papa's Letter (page 4)

David's Wedding, 2003

Herr Müller, 2007

Drancy Memorial

Front Page *NY Post*

Papa's House, Stattsoper Berlin

My Milton

Baby David and Me

Rita, 19 and Engaged

Good-bye Dinner with Mademoiselle

Daddy Sam and Aunt Gerdy

My five-year-old brother,
Michel

Princess Bride and Jack, her Prince

Nay, France 1942 (from left: Rita, Papa, Susi, Mama, Sylvia)

Tragic Day in Rivesaltes, 1942 (upper left: half-hidden face Lisl
Hanau; top right: nine-year-old Susi; bottom row left: three-year-old
Sylvie; behind me is ten-year-old Rita.)

Mama and Papa Together Again (Stolpersteine.)

ACKNOWLEDGMENTS

This book took a long time and a lot of people helped me along the way.

The emotional staying power I needed to tell this story came from several sources. For their sustained encouragement and feedback, my great thanks to Audrey Mei, Dyan deNapoli, my "Goddess" Kate Victory Hannisian, and my soul sister Ishy Creo.

For their invaluable feedback I am so grateful to my early readers, Mona Pearl Treyball, Betsy Anthony, and Minda Cedano.

Thank you Alan Rinzler for helping to keep my butt in the chair.

Thanks to David Aretha for his excellent editorial guidance.

To Vera Kaplan my deepest gratitude. For everything.

Thank you to the Holocaust Survivors Oral Health Program for my amazing dentists Drs. Arvi and Adelina Duka, who provide me with free, expert care. I am blessed by their kindness and grace.

A heartfelt thank you to the many generous donors who were moved by my story. I am a lucky woman.

No one wanted to publish this story. But then the Universe gave me a gift. Thank you to Paul Cohen and Colin Rolfe of Monkfish/Epigraph Publishing for finally bringing this book out in the world.

My thanks to Meryl Zegarek, my publicist, who knows everyone a fledgling author should meet.

To my "Duvy," my David, my warrior king, my son. This book is for you!

CPSIA information can be obtained
at www.ICGtesting.com
Printed in the USA
FSHW02n2010050818
51185FS

9 781944 037949